the Winemaker

the
Winemaker

George
Fistonich
and the
Villa Maria
Story

Kerry R Tyack

RANDOM HOUSE
NEW ZEALAND

A RANDOM HOUSE BOOK published by Random House New Zealand
18 Poland Road, Glenfield, Auckland, New Zealand

For more information about our titles go to www.randomhouse.co.nz

A catalogue record for this book is available from the National Library
of New Zealand

Random House New Zealand is part of the Random House Group
New York   London   Sydney   Auckland   Delhi   Johannesburg

First published 2012
This hardback edition published 2012

© 2012 Kerry R Tyack; photographs: Jane Ussher pp 2–3, 6–7, 12–13, 26–27,
46–47, 58–59, 70–71, 86–87, 112–113, 130–131, 152–153, 162–163, 176–177,
194–195, 220–221, 238–239, 250–251, 268–269, 290–291, 301, 306, 312–313,
332–333, 342–343; Richard Brimer pp 223, 245, 247, 249, 267, 275; Jeremy
and Judy Waldron p 229; all other images from the Fistonich family and
Villa Maria collections

The moral rights of the author have been asserted

ISBN 978 1 92715 814 2

Design: Carla Sy
Front cover image: Jane Ussher

Printed in China by Everbest Printing Co Ltd

TO GAIL; TO MY CHILDREN, KAREN, MICHAEL AND MEGAN;
AND TO MY GRANDCHILDREN, BENJAMIN, OLIVIA,
MATTHEW, MILAN, ANNA AND KATIE

— George Fistonich

TO MY SONS, OLIVER AND FINDLAY

— Kerry Tyack

SKILL PATIENCE DEDICATION

VILLA MAR
CABERNET SAUV
1985

...od matured dry red produced
...grown grapes. Further cellari...
...softness and complexity is...
Serve at room temperatu...

CONTENTS

PRELUDE

September 2011. The Hilton Hotel, Park Lane, London. For over an hour, taxis and limos had been depositing Masters of Wine, leading wine merchants and members of the wine trade at the hotel steps. Women in evening dress, men in tuxedos. It was the culmination of the 2011 International Wine Challenge.

The tables in the vast ballroom had steadily filled with a who's who of the industry, 700 people in all. This was the night when Merchant of the Year and Winemaker of the Year would be announced, when the highly anticipated decisions of the team of international wine judges would be made public.

When the website for the challenge stated that it had brought together some of the most important people in the wine world, and that this was 'probably the biggest wine competition in the world', it wasn't kidding. The challenge, first held in 1984, was jointly chaired by Charles Metcalfe, Derek Smedley MW, Tim Atkin MW and Sam Harrop MW, and involved many stars of the international wine industry. The 2011 challenge had involved 24 panel chairs, the vast bulk of them Masters of Wine, the others a collection of esteemed wine writers, winemakers, scientists and wine marketers. They had been assisted by 59 senior judges, 125 judges and 97 associate judges from around the world.

New Zealand had been honoured here before, and as he took his seat George Fistonich was quietly hopeful that a Villa Maria wine would once again take one of the trophies. When the 2007 Villa Maria Single Vineyard Taylors Pass Chardonnay got the nod he smiled broadly. Excellent. It was a wine he and his team rated highly. The vineyard lay on the north side of the Awatere in Marlborough, and when he had bought the land in 1998 he had always imagined that it would one day deliver a perfect Chardonnay.

The evening drew to an end at around 11.45pm. There had been a constant stream of awards recognising the best of the British wine and spirit trade. There had been no speeches, but even so it had been a long night: 89 champion trophy results; 94 trophy winners. It came time for individuals of the wine industry to be honoured. The big award would be the IWC Lifetime Achievement Award. In 2010 the winner had been the Spaniard Miguel Torres, who joined the three-century-old family company Bodega Torres in 1962 and currently serves as its president and CEO. The year before that the honour had gone to Peter Lehmann, who founded Peter Lehmann Wines in 1979 and who has been described as one of Australia's most respected and innovative winemakers. A short video was played. The room went quiet.

'And the IWC Lifetime Achievement Award goes to George Fistonich of Villa Maria Wines!' the MC was saying, as the room erupted into applause. It was hard to credit. Villa Maria's UK market manager Penny Fear, who was sitting next to George, was beaming in delight. George pushed his chair back from the table and straightened his bow-tie as he walked up to the podium, threading his way through the tables. He hadn't prepared a speech, but somehow he managed to collect his thoughts so he could acknowledge how Villa's exports to the United Kingdom about 25 years earlier 'really were the beginning of our export success'.

He thanked Patrick McGrath from Hatch Mansfield, Villa Maria's long-time agency in the United Kingdom, and made sure to thank 'all who have supported us over the years', including the always-important wine merchants and supermarkets who stocked Villa wines. It was off-the-cuff, but it was received with a standing ovation. George felt comfortable he hadn't missed anyone out. This was important.

He knew people had long memories when it came to recognition, or lack of it.

As he made his way back to the table, George felt a mix of emotions: delight, surprise, pride. He thought of the Villa Maria team back at the winery in Mangere, the board, the winemakers and viticulturists in Hawke's Bay and Marlborough, the reps on the road. How thrilled they would be. How thrilled he was, not so much for himself, but for Villa Maria. It was one more honour and one more validation that he could bestow on the company, as he had been working so hard to do for 50 years. One more gong, one more honour. Like the 2009 knighthood and the countless trophies . . . it was all for Villa Maria, for the team and the staff. Always had been. Always would be.

1

A LAND OF PROMISE

In 1926 a young Croatian named Andrija Fistonich stepped off a ship onto the Auckland wharves after three months at sea. He had boarded the ship at Genoa, and it had travelled through the ports of southern Europe, stopping to restock in South East Asia. In 1926 Auckland was a very small city, but it seemed vast compared to his little village of Zastražišće on the island of Otok Hvar, which lay just off the coast from what was then Yugoslavia.

Andrija Fistonich, standing at far right,
with fellow gumdiggers in Northland.

Andrija was keen to see his new country. He had cousins here, and their letters home had filled him with images of a land with a mild climate and fertile soils, of a modern, progressive, democratic society far removed from his homeland, which had for so long been the pawn of the imperial aspirations of its neighbours.

His cousin Andrija Zencic showed him around Auckland, and within days Andrija had found room and board with a Mr and Mrs Lavas, who had a large house on Hobson Street. These days Hobson Street is choked with motorway-bound traffic, but back then it was a suburb contiguous with Freemans Bay, full of old houses, Chinese shops, and churches and schools. Economically it was on the slide, as so many of Auckland's very early suburbs were, and the area was full of new migrants, including a large number of Dalmatian — as Croatians were then usually known — families.

Finding work was a matter of urgency for Andrija, and it wasn't going to be easy for an immigrant with no English and no money. Not for the first time in his life, the Dalmatian network helped him out. Andrija Zencic found work for him in the quarry on Rangitoto Island; it proved grindingly tough work, chipping away all day at the island's scoria rock under a blazing sun. After a couple of months, Andrija decided to move north, to where so many of his countrymen were labouring — on the Northland gum fields. There, the gumdiggers lived in rough camps, and digging up fallen kauri trees to find the clumps of solidified gum was hard and monotonous work. However, during that time Andrija's English started to develop slowly, as he learned the language from the Catholic missionaries in the area.

After five hard years in the north, Andrija moved again, this time south to Ngatea, to work on a drainage scheme on the Hauraki Plains, before a job came up at the Horotiu freezing works on the northern outskirts of Hamilton. Along the way Andrija made contact with two more Fistonich cousins: his namesake, another Andrija Fistonich, who had originally gone to work near Whangarei but who later settled in Oratia, and Mate, who had settled in Titirangi. The associations with the Dalmatian community, and especially with those from Zastražišće or from close by, bound him tightly and supported him greatly. By the time he returned to Auckland in 1935 he had money saved, and sufficient prospects that a woman might consider him a suitable husband. The community would be involved in that, too.

Mandica Banovich came from the village of Gdinj, also on Otok Hvar. Eager for her daughter to have a better life, Mandica's mother had sought the help of her eldest daughter Stefica, who had married her mother's cousin George Popovic, a well-to-do Croatian who owned the Delta Picture Theatre in New Lynn, in Auckland's western suburbs. At the request of her mother, Stefica and George sponsored Mandica to come to New Zealand. A new life was mapped out for her: she would find a husband, have children, and make a better life in the new country.

Mandica lived with the Popovics, earning her board by helping a Mrs Sokolich, who lived in Fruitvale Road, New Lynn, with her young family. It was her brother-in-law's job to find Mandica a suitable suitor from among the many unmarried young male immigrants from Dalmatia. Time was of the essence: New Zealand immigration law determined that 'aliens' had to marry within three months of their arrival or risk being sent home again. George and Stefica introduced Mandica to their friend Mick Radja. She liked Mick but he had health problems, and she felt it would be better to search instead for someone with better prospects.

No one now can quite remember how Mandica and Andrija met, but once they had it was clear that she would not be marrying Mick

Radja. Mandica struck Andrija as hardworking, intelligent, and responsible. For her part, she could see him as a husband to rely on. In 1935, at the age of 28, she married 36-year-old Andrija Fistonich at St Patrick's Cathedral, with Andrija's sister, Antica, and Stefica as bridesmaids, their husbands as groomsmen, and Antica's daughter Kathy as flower girl.

THE CROATIAN IMMIGRANTS bought land. It was what you did; how you put down new roots in a new land that would grow deep. Mandica and Andrija decided they would buy their land not out in West Auckland, where so many Croatians had settled, but rather near Mangere mountain. Andrija's sister Antica was already living here with her husband Grgo (George) Babich, on a five-acre block opposite the cemetery. Andrija and Mandica could see, from the area's well-kept farms and market gardens, that the soil there was fertile, the climate mild, and the locals hardworking. Five acres on Kirkbride Road were for sale for £500. It was not the hard, barren Yugoslav soil of Andrija's youth, but rich, fertile volcanic soil that had been thrown up by the mountain many ages before. As they stood looking at the plot, Mandica and Andrija could see their future unfolding. They would live and raise a family here. Food would be plentiful. There would be a couple of cows, some sheep, lots of hens. A vineyard would flourish that they would name Mountain Vineyards, growing grapes the way Andrija had learned in Yugoslavia, with help at harvest and vintage coming from other Croatians. They would have a prolific orchard with abundant apples, peaches and citrus fruit, and they would plant corn and beans and make wine. Their children would have a better life than they had had. The immigrants' dream would be fulfilled.

While their modest home was being built, they lived with Grgo and Antica and helped them on their property while also preparing their own land for planting. By this time Grgo had established his own small vineyard, which later, at the start of the Second World War, would become popular as a gathering place for American servicemen based in Mangere.

Mandica Fistonich with George outside the
house she and Andrija built on Kirkbride
Road in Mangere.

Creating a better future was vitally important to Andrija. He was mostly a happy man who loved to socialise with neighbours and Croatian friends in West Auckland, but he was also a man who deeply regretted not having had a better education. He would have loved to have gone to university and be further educated. On Otok Hvar there had been only a very basic school; if families wanted to further their children's education they would have to travel off the island to one of the cities on the mainland, usually the town of Split, but sometimes much further afield. There were not many families who had the wherewithal to send their children away.

And having a plot of land was vital for Mandica. If Andrija was intellectual, a man who loved reading and reciting history, and arguing with the priests when they came to visit, a man who only ever went to church on Christmas Day and possibly Easter Sunday, then Mandica was more suited to owning and working a patch of land. She was more down-to-earth, more work-orientated.

In this family, hard work, thrift, drive and family loyalty were to be paramount. The children would be encouraged to do well at school, and to maintain the Croatian language at home. They would be expected to work the land with their parents; and right from the start it was George who would show the most interest in the land. He was always there to help.

THERE WERE FOUR children, Elsie, Ivan, George (born on 23 November 1939, at St Margaret's Hospital in Epsom, Auckland), and then Peter, born eight years after George. The children's uncle and aunt, George and Stefica Popovic, couldn't have children and wanted to adopt. When Ivan was born, they had come to see Andrija and Mandica to ask for the child. They had sponsored Mandica, and so there was a sense of obligation. Andrija and Mandica would never consider their eldest son being taken, however, and the Popovics didn't want a girl, so when Elsie had come along earlier she was never considered. George? The boy who would come to be the Fistonich child most keen on working the family land, the son so close to his mother? Yes, possibly George. But George was eight when they asked for him, and he kicked up a fuss.

So it was the youngest, Peter, who would leave Mangere and become Peter Popovic when just an infant. It was an open adoption; Ivan, Elsie and George clearly identified Peter as their sibling. But the adoption bothered Peter as he got older; perhaps that is why, George now thinks, Peter could never quite settle to anything, including life as a lawyer after graduating from law school.

Andrija, who was 41 when George was born and working as night-watchman at the AFFCO meat works in Westfield, had his children's lives mapped out for them. They knew what they needed to be, as he told them often: Ivan a lawyer, George a tradesman, and Elsie a married woman, which she did indeed become. In April 1955, at St Patrick's Cathedral, when she was only 17, Elsie married Frank Yukich, who would later establish Montana Wines. Elsie and Frank would have six children, all born relatively close together; the marriage ended 17 years later, and she subsequently remarried and is now Elsie Thom.

Ivan, who was to die in 1998, aged 59, was a lot like his father. Clever, intellectual, occasionally temperamental, always sociable and the life and soul of the party, he had huge charisma, huge empathy. If he was in a good mood, he would light up the room. If he was in a bad mood, you got out of his way. He was hugely artistic and talented: he could draw and paint, design houses — and indeed he designed one for his parents — and was a great gardener. Ivan proved a good lawyer, and he did reasonably well at it, mainly as a result of the great empathy he had with his clients, many of whom were devoted to him, but his natural talents probably would have had a more rewarding outlet had he been an architect or a painter. That wasn't Andrija's vision at all.

Money was always scarce in the household, especially during the war and after, well on into the 1950s. Andrija had his full-time work at the freezing works, but it was not enough. Mandica bartered with Mr Evans, the grocer at Mangere Bridge, using her eggs and vegetables to keep costs down and pay for most of the essentials.

ABOVE

Mandica and Andrija Fistonich with the
children. Elsie is standing at left. In the
front, from left, are George, Peter and Ivan.

She also had a milk-separator and sold cream to a milk factory that collected it from the gate.

There was no radio — and TV had yet to appear in New Zealand — although when George was about 10 or 11 years old the family got a homemade radio, a big yellow box, built by the man who used to operate the film-projector at George Popovic's cinema.

A Russian neighbour, Mr Matieoff, had a market garden, and when he needed help to pick his prolific crop of vegetables, Ivan, Elsie and George were sent to work, being paid three shillings for a large case of tomatoes, five shillings for a large case of peas, and two shillings and sixpence for beans. It was hard work. The children regarded Mr Matieoff as very old. He had a large, droopy moustache, was somewhat bandy-legged, and was always in old clothes, so they were shocked when he brought home a young bride and a child. It seemed so wrong: he must have been nearly 40 by this time, and therefore close to death in their eyes. Why he had married was beyond their comprehension. Years later they realised that his wife was probably a war refugee with a very sad history.

The Fistonich children supplemented the family coffers by hunting for mushrooms across nearby paddocks. They were free to go anywhere, as all the neighbours were considered friends and there were no harmful sprays on the fields in those days. The mushrooms were sold to a fruiterer in Onehunga for a nice return. Mandica also sent them blackberry-picking in the gullies that ran down to the Manukau beaches.

EVERYTHING ABOUT the family was disciplined. If the children wanted fivepence to go to the pictures on a Saturday afternoon or wanted an ice-cream, they had to work to earn it. They had to dig the garden, mow the lawn, and do chores for three to four hours a day. George was hand-milking cows morning and night at the age of 10. There were roughly two acres of grazing for the cows, an acre of market garden, an acre of grapes and an acre of fruit trees, so there was always a lot of digging and weeding.

As the grapes ripened, their father would call them to 'get outside and shake the tins', and the children would run out to rattle the line of empty cans that their parents had strung the length of the vineyard. The children would spend hours trudging up and down the rows, rattling the tins to keep away the birds: sparrows, white-eyes, thrushes and blackbirds which, if not fought off, would decimate the grapes in a day. It was a dreary task and one they disliked, but Andrija would not tolerate any dissension. The Fistonich children felt their parents were very strict. None of their friends seemed to have to work, they just got pocket money!

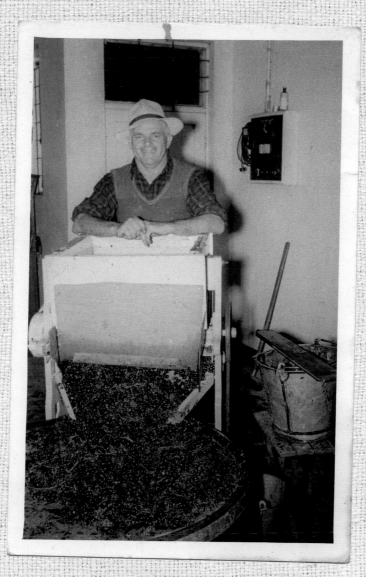

Andrija Fistonich in the Mountain
Vineyards winery, using the homemade
grape-crusher built for him by a neighbour,
Viv Wright, by constructing a box around
a washing-machine clothes press and
strapping wires to the rollers.

2
A MANGERE
UPBRINGING

Despite the lack of money and the ever-present emphasis on work, the Fistonichs' childhood in Mangere was happy and healthy. Mangere was almost all farmland, a friendly community where people knew and helped one another. All the locals enjoyed the outdoors, so a good deal of time was spent exploring the local countryside; one of the favourite places was Ihumatao, near the local Maori pa where the family had some friends. Some of those paddocks are now part of Villa Maria.

Mandica (centre), Elsie
(right) and a friend at
harvest time.

A beach just down Creamery Road, not far from the Fistonich home, was called Ambury's after the disused dairy factory on its shores. It was a popular playground for local children, who were almost always totally unsupervised and yet survived many adventures. Groups of them would explore the old factory, initially breaking in, curious to see inside. They would drag the old dinghies that were pulled up on the beach down to the water, and were lucky never to sink them. They would fish for flounder, and gather oysters and scallops and crabs by the sackful. The Mangere sewage treatment plant was yet to be built, and the water was clean and fresh seafood abundant. Later, when he was an apprentice, George would take sacks of oyster or scallops as a treat for his workmates.

Very few neighbours had cars. Rather, the Mangere locals used the bus service that passed the cemetery and went along Coronation Road, or they would walk the other way to Blackbridge. The Fistonich children often trudged the 45 minutes from Mangere to Onehunga. There were always distractions along the way and it never seemed that long.

As they grew older they were given bikes, and on weekends they would bike everywhere, sometimes even as far as West Auckland to see friends. If they were going to Onehunga or the city on the bus, their bikes could be left safely in a paddock at Blackbridge all day. Later, George would bike to and from high school, at De La Salle

Mandica and the family's pride and joy,
their first car, a Ford Prefect.

College in Mangere East, every day. And no matter how badly they scraped their knees and legs, Mandica's cure of mashed herbs from the garden — often mixed with the fiery Croatian liquor rakija or Rawleigh's ointment — almost always worked. If something stronger *was* required, Mandica would delve into her cherished medical books to find out how to make a potion she thought would fix the problem.

THE FAMILY SELDOM had holidays. Mandica and Andrija were always saving for something or other, and there was never much money left for getting away from the property. That changed somewhat when, at 50, Andrija finally got his driver's licence and the family got its first car. By then George was aged around 12 and attending St Peter's College, in Mount Eden. Andrija had bought a brand-new Ford Prefect, and on the day he took ownership he proudly drove it to St Peter's to collect the boys from school. They watched in horror as right outside the school he turned too sharply and drove into the side of a tram, scratching one side of the car.

The kids would pile into the car for dusty road-trips up to Kaitaia, to visit friends in the big Croatian community there. Occasionally they would go and visit their relations the Devcichs, who lived up the Kauaeranga Valley just out of Thames.

Many of the most special times in the family's life involved George's uncle and aunt Popovic from New Lynn. A family lunch with their aunt and uncle was a regular Sunday ritual. Their uncle had quite a bit of say in the lives of the Mangere Fistonichs, which George remembers as not always being a positive thing, but that was the way of family. George and Stefica had a car well before Andrija bought his, and the children would go off with Uncle George, carrying several sacks to collect oysters and pipi from the causeway to Puketutu Island. They would also go to Ihumatao, where George Popovic had permission to go across paddocks on some of the farms. There, there were very large colourful crabs to catch, and they would drag big sacks of shellfish back to the house, for Mandica to boil in the copper. Then the neighbours, the Masseys, would come over to join in a big meal with lots of bread and butter and wine.

George Popovic was very interested in carrier pigeons and decided to train them to fly from his loft in New Lynn to a shed Andrija had on the property in Mangere. It worked well until Mandica got tired of the pigeon droppings and called a stop to the cross-isthmus flights. Another room in the shed had been set aside as a playroom for the children, and George papered its walls with promotional posters of Betty Grable, John Wayne, Clarke Gable, Greer Garson and other film stars of the time that his uncle brought from his movie theatre.

Not far from the house was a huge shed. During the war, George Popovic decided he could get extra petrol if he hid one of his cars at Andrija and Mandica's property, passing it off as the Fistonichs' to get extra petrol rations. There was a large holding of fowls and a rooster in an adjoining building, and one day they escaped, found the car and perched all over it. Somehow Andrija and Mandica missed this intrusion, and when George next came around there was a huge row. Away the car went, and along with it — to the children's joy — Uncle George's huge barrel of sauerkraut. They hated the vinegary taste of the cabbage. Peace was eventually restored and George and Stefica continued to play a large part in their lives.

Andrija and Mandica were very proud of their children, and every so often would take the family to the local studio where they would have photographs taken to send back to the grandparents in Yugoslavia. On one of these visits, George was determined not to be photographed. It took a stern warning from his father to win his co-operation, and close examination of the subsequent photograph reveals faint traces of tears of rage on his face and his curly hair in disarray.

AT THE TIME it was illegal to produce rakija, the fiery liquid that Croatians considered a necessity for curing most ailments, but that didn't stop Andrija and Mandica, who made theirs in the washhouse. The still was part of the copper, its pipes reaching outside. When their parents were brewing a batch, the children kept lookout, taking

Mandica Fistonich, far right, with her sister
Stefica Popovic and her brother-in-law
George Popovic.

turns to sit on the gate at the intersection of Mountain, Creamery and Kirkbride roads, to watch out for the local policeman, Mr Watts, who lived just along Mountain Road and who would often call in to see them. They could see his green car as it cruised down from the top of Mountain Road, and if it did not turn into his own driveway they would jump down and run to warn their parents. Once he got so close that they had to distract him so he didn't go through the small front gate. Looking back, George is sure that Watts knew what was going on but decided to turn a blind eye. That Mrs Watts was Croatian may have had something to do with it; she was pleased to receive the odd bottle of cooking sherry from Andrija.

In this era, regulations governing the sale of alcohol were very strict, and included the requirement that all brandy used to fortify sherry and port be held in bond by Customs, to be portioned out sparingly. This led many winemakers — Andrija and Mandica among them — to make their own fortifying spirit illegally. Very few were caught.

Despite living in Mangere, the Fistonich family maintained strong ties with the West Auckland Croatians, including the Babich, Lendich, Delegat, Selak, Fredatovich and Buljan families. Big family social gatherings were relatively frequent, and provided an important opportunity to share their culture and language. Many of Auckland's Croatian families had come out from the same villages in Croatia, and many were related. For example, Mrs Delegat and Mrs Selak were brother and sister. It was a community full of great characters; the children learned to be in awe of Joe Babich senior — father of Joe and Peter — who was considered a godfather in the district, and of the highly respected Nicola Delegat.

Discussions and conversations would be conducted in Croatian, which the Fistonich children took in their stride. They all spoke the language fluently, to the extent that George didn't speak English until he was five years old. (He spoke in Croatian with his parents until he was in his late teens.) But the use of the language was even then starting to diminish for New Zealand-born Croatians; the Fistonichs were unusual in speaking Croatian as often as they did.

In the 1950s, New Zealand's Croatian winemakers held
an annual dinner to which government ministers and
officials were invited. Their sons and their friends (many
of whom were from orchards in the Henderson Valley)
were placed in charge of the tables, pouring the wine and
answering questions. Shown with then Prime Minister
Sir Walter Nash are, from left, Ivan Posa, George Fistonich,
Johnny Sutich, Joe Babich, Anthony Udjur, Filip Babich,
Clem Erceg and Barry Sunde.

GEORGE BEGAN SCHOOL at the local primary in Mangere Bridge, but when he was eight his parents decided to send the children across the Manukau Harbour to Onehunga, to St Joseph's Convent School in Church Street, where they felt the children would benefit from the religious focus provided by the teaching nuns. It was quite a hike; the roads were gravel, and the Fistonich children kept to the grass on the road edge.

On very wet days they would wonder if Mr Kelliher would stop and give them a lift. Mr Kelliher (later Sir Henry Kelliher) lived in a grand house on Puketutu Island, which sits in the Manukau Harbour. The Fistonich children knew he owned a brewery (Dominion Breweries) and that he was very rich. Sometimes his big car stopped, and there was always great disappointment when it did not. The wondering could be a bit nerve-wracking, George remembers. The kids loved his huge, flash Packard. He would pile them all into the back — no seat belts then.

One particular day, Kelliher stopped and the kids clambered into the back. However, that day the brewery magnate must have had a lot on his mind, because he sailed on past the school until someone let out a yelp. He stopped a little further on, down by the shops, and they were not given a lift again.

In Form One, George had been sent to St Peter's College. However, halfway through his third form year, Bishop Liston, the Catholic Bishop of Auckland, ordered all students who lived south of the Manukau Harbour bridge to transfer to a new school, De La Salle, which had just been built in Mangere East. George missed St Peter's a good deal. The 70 to 80 boys in his year were like a community; the boys came from right across Auckland, including from St Joseph's. At De La Salle many of the pupils were from south of Auckland, as far away as Pukekohe.

Strangely, given the enthusiasm George's parents had for education, reading was not actively encouraged in the Fistonich home. Andrija and Mandica didn't much believe in children spending time with books, perhaps in case they read the wrong things. George grabbed the occasional comic or magazine, and later graduated to

George drives the rotary hoe,
towing bushel cases of grapes. His
friend Dennis Kosijer leans on the
boxes of grapes on the trailer.

Agatha Christie and Merlin mysteries, as well as Alfred Hitchcock stories, 'but off my own bat, not because I was made to'.

He was a competent sportsman, who sometimes had to resort to subterfuge in order to indulge his passion for rugby, as Mandica and Andrija were very much against the game. They thought it was dangerous, and that sport in general was an indulgence. In their view, George would be better off spending the time working. If he had a Saturday rugby game, George had to pretend he was going elsewhere and then somehow sneak in and wash his clothes and clean his boots afterwards. He also played soccer and did athletics. He was a reasonably good sprinter, with strong legs, and because of all his bike-riding he was also a pretty good cyclist.

George was also keen on cars and motorbikes. When he was 17 he bought a motorbike, much to his father's disapproval. By then he had been working for a couple of years and had a bit of disposable cash, and he decided a motorbike was a logical way of dealing with Auckland traffic. And it couldn't have hurt in attracting the attention of girls.

THE FISTONICH CHILDREN were brought up strictly, but not in a suffocatingly religious way. Mandica was the more spiritual of the parents, and insisted the children went to the Church of Our Lady of the Assumption in Onehunga every Sunday, and to confession every Saturday. Andrija enjoyed church more for the ritual of the services than anything else, and was an infrequent attendee. When he did go to Mass he would always linger after service, eager for an opportunity to debate with the priest. At 11, Ivan entered the Holy Cross seminary in Mosgiel to train for the priesthood. After four years there he decided it was not the life for him and he returned to Auckland, where he would eventually attend law school.

The family was dutiful in its Catholicism rather than pious, but, even so, George remembers the 1950s as 'an era when people were very indoctrinated by the church. At De La Salle we had to stand up every Monday and declare if we had been to church the day before and if you hadn't, you got a belt.

'Elsie religiously went to church every week right until she had the last of her six kids. She suddenly decided she didn't want to have any more kids and went to three different priests for advice and got three different answers. One elderly Irish priest said, you have done your duty so you don't need to have any more kids, just practise safe sex. Another priest told her she had done her duty, to not worry about it and to start using contraception, and another priest told her something else. So she thought "bugger this" and from that point on her commitment to the Church waned a little and she went to Church less frequently.'

George kept going to church until he left school, but well before that he had started to question what were supposedly immutable rules. 'At one point you weren't allowed to eat meat on a Friday, and then the rules changed and you could eat meat on a Friday. We had always been told it was a "God rule" and I thought, "How can you change a 'God rule'?"'

The doubts began to grow. 'I even started to question priests. People seemed to believe that it was wrong to ask questions, and if you did they would turn off, would not give you answers. In the end I was probably influenced by the fact that if you walked down the street and looked at all the pretty girls and thought they were desirable, then you were sinning. If you thought a bit further, then it could be a mortal sin . . . I started to question all this. Over time I became disillusioned and stopped going to church, and I stopped taking communion. I suppose as far as the Catholic Church was concerned, there were things I was doing that I wasn't meant to do — like taking out girls!'

This propensity to ask questions and be curious about life has stayed with George all his life. 'Don't get me wrong, I respect religion, hugely, but I have never accepted blind faith. I believe we all have a right to ask questions and get answers.'

UNIVERSITY WAS NEVER going to be an option for George Fistonich. 'The way the Fistonich Croatian family worked was that the older son went to university and the younger son was expected to do a trade. It was a matter of great pride to my father that he had saved enough money and could send my older brother to university to do law. But there was never any discussion about me following him; it was always going to be a trade for me.' So in 1955, after George turned 15, he left De La Salle College and began what was anticipated to be a five-year building apprenticeship with H J Short & Company, a large, well-respected company with around 50 to 60 staff. H J Short began in housing and then moved on to larger commercial building projects such as the Onehunga Hotel and the Ranfurly War Veterans' Home in Mount Roskill, projects that were considered reasonably large-scale at the time.

Henry Short was an influential businessman in Mangere. He and his wife, Viola, were very social, highly respected local citizens. The garden parties at their lavish property opposite Mangere Bridge School were legendary. Viola Short had her own radio programme, where she talked about gardening, and Henry Short was a member of the local Mangere Bridge Council.

When George first went to see Short about a job, Short told him he would get him work on housing, where he could learn the carpentry trade. For the first year George worked in the workshop doing joinery, making window frames and kitchen cabinets. It soon became apparent that he was a perfectionist at hanging doors, and there was never any doubt that he would complete his apprenticeship: 'You did what your parents told you.'

After about a year, George asked Short if he could move to a housing job, and some time later he was assigned to the Ranfurly War Veterans' Home project. On the first day on site a carpenter asked, 'You are the new apprentice, are you? Pick up that bit of timber. No, tell you what. You've got a bucket . . . fill it up with some nails over at that shed over there. Pick up a plank of 4 x 2 and pretend you are looking busy . . . Pick it up, put it down, look busy, don't get caught.'

George, not his hardworking parents' son for nothing, was appalled and was on the verge of handing in his notice. A little later he was transferred to the Onehunga Hotel site, where he once again

Ivan, left, and George
Fistonich in the
traditional Croatian
costume for performing
the kolo dance.

found himself frustrated. There was strong union control of the building industry, and the unions were dominated by a lot of English immigrants. 'There were four or five apprentices, and we all seemed to be just mucking around pouring concrete. We all used to play poker at morning tea, and I remember one day a whole gang of us got into the basement . . . and we actually played poker all day and nobody missed us! If there was no concrete pouring we just seemed to be filling in time. I said to the other apprentices, "You guys are mad, you are going to come out of this knowing nothing". I suppose it was my first time of being independent and I was not prepared to waste my time and future, learning nothing on apprentices' starting wages.'

At the time George was earning £3 13/- a week. 'It started getting intolerable, so I went and saw Henry Short and told him what I thought of what I was being told to do, that I had learned absolutely nothing and that I wanted to transfer to be a house builder. Well, apparently that caused a huge disruption . . . I was called into his office and he said, "Look, we will put you on a better wage and put you on the next housing project that comes along."'

True to his word, Short gave George a pay-rise, made him a leading hand, and set him to work on his own Mangere property, building fences and working around the garden helping Viola. But by this stage George had already made up his mind that he was going to change his employer. 'Many of the guys I had gone through with and studied with at Short would not have known how to independently build a house or do joinery or anything in a reasonable time,' he says. 'So I went to the local apprenticeship committee and asked for a transfer. Nothing happened at first, but eventually I got transferred to Merv Bowden, a luxury home builder.

'Even there the staff used to take up to half an hour for morning tea and sometimes about an hour for lunch. Bowden was an extremely good builder; we did fantastic work, everything was very precise, very high-quality.' But George felt the staff had an overly relaxed attitude to work hours, and the houses invariably ran over budget. However, after 18 months Bowden ran into financial difficulties and had to close down, and George transferred and

Mandica picking grapes
on the Mangere property.

completed his apprenticeship with Lloyd Hotchin, the builder of more basic houses, from whom he learned to work at great speed; the company was completing a house every two months.

But by now he had decided he wanted to get out of building, so he studied for the building trade certificate in order to get six months off his apprenticeship. It took him three years of going to night-school to complete it. Almost 300 apprentices started with him, but, while many of them loved their trade, very few of them would go on to complete their qualifications. 'On the other hand, they were natural, dedicated tradesmen,' he says now. 'Many would do well.'

'I got another six months off for getting my School Cert before I started, then I got another two months off because I had done quite a significant amount of overtime and completed 10,000 hours,' he remembers. He had completed his five-year apprenticeship in three years and 10 months. At the age of 20, he was now building on his own account — alterations, a couple of garages, and sheds. And he was also helping Andrija at the vineyard, in the orchard, and milking the two house cows.

Andrija was in his late fifties and, despite suffering chronic asthma, was still relatively fit and strong; the chronic illness that would eventually force him to stop work had not yet appeared. George welcomed the work in the vineyard. He had come to realise that building was not the trade for him: that he was not patient and tolerant enough, and that he didn't easily cope with doing the same thing over and over without boredom creeping in. In spite of a natural aptitude for the trade, it offered him no challenge and did not suit his restless nature. But he had set his mind to earn his apprenticeship, and he had done it.

3
THE WINEMAKER

In the New Zealand of George Fistonich's youth there was really only one drink for men: beer. While women drank sherry and would have a shandy or spirit cocktail in the Ladies' Bar at the local hotel, it was nonetheless predominantly a beer nation. But if you were Croatian you drank wine, which proved highly problematic. In a country dominated by the breweries, winemaking was essentially limited to small home-based winemakers and a few more substantial wineries scattered throughout the country. It was almost an underground activity.

Ivan Ivankovich pruning
on the Fistonich property.

D espite the fact that the wine had been made in New Zealand right back in the time when James Busby was the British Government's Resident at Waitangi, in 1840, the Temperance movement of the 1890s and the power of the breweries had ensured that by the 1920s only a handful of communities of Catholic priests seemed to know how to grow grapes and make wine. The Croatians had pretty soon figured out that if they wanted wine they would have to make their own.

The wine made by Andrija at Kirkbride Road — with, it must be said, plenty of involvement from Mandica, who had a more natural feel for winemaking — was intended primarily for the family's own use. But in 1948 the government, which had previously been at worst hostile and at best ambivalent about the local wine industry, introduced a licence which allowed grape growers to establish retail outlets on their properties and to make a little extra revenue from the sale of their wine.

Andrija saw his chance, and in 1944 he hired local builder Bill Laing to build a 900-square-foot building on the corner of Creamery and Kirkbride roads. (He had it built in the shape of a house, with the requisite doors and windows, so it could be converted into a house should the winery ever be closed down. Years later it would be converted into the Villa Maria caretaker's residence, and it still stands today.)

In order to gain a licence and to be able to sell their wine legally, Andrija and Mandica registered their winery as Mountain Vineyards. The children now had vineyard work added to their already long list of chores: they were set to work weeding under the vines and washing the bottles by hand.

In addition to dry red wine for their own use, Andrija and Mandica Fistonich, like all the other Croatian winemaking families, made port and sherry for the locals who liked the sweeter styles. Andrija and Mandica were very hospitable, and if customers were not in a hurry they would be welcomed into the kitchen to sit for a while and have a drink. One of the regulars was a Maori man from the cluster of Maori-owned houses further round the mountain that local Pakeha called 'the Pa'. The Fistonich children dubbed him 'broken-voice Charlie' on account of his very unusual voice. He always came with a very refined Maori woman, whom the Fistonichs were not sure was his wife or his daughter.

Selling wine on Sundays and after 9pm was illegal, and although the still-fledgling wine industry had to accept these strictures there were plenty of clandestine sales. At the time the only other source of wine was the brewery-dominated wine stores, which, because of what was known as 'tied-house status', were limited to selling the wines determined by the brewery owners. At this time Andrija was working full-time as a night-watchman on the Auckland wharves. Customers would drop in at night when Andrija was at work, often rapping on the bedroom window. If Mandica was unwell and in bed, one of the children would pass out the wine, collect the money and then go back to bed.

But when Andrija was there he was emphatically in charge. One day he caught someone stealing, and chased after him with the double-barrelled shotgun Ivan and George used for shooting birds in the vineyard. Fortunately, the gun jammed or the Fistonich family may have had an embarrassment on its hands.

In 1956 Andrija decided to travel to Yugoslavia for six months to see his elderly father, whom he had not seen since he had left the country in 1926. While he was away, George, recently into his apprenticeship, would help his mother at the winery, and with his mother's support he made a few changes that Andrija, on his return, would question but not alter.

ALL THIS TIME, George was moving towards a decision to begin making wine on his own account. How could he not, growing up in a world where many of one's Croatian friends and relations made wine, drank wine, compared wine notes? Whether at Mountain Vineyards, at the Montana winery or out at the Babichs', the Selaks' and the Delegats', or at the Croatian Club, they drank each other's wines, talked about each other's wines. Throughout Henderson — often referred to as Dally Valley — and nearby Kumeu, there were between 80 and 90 wineries. Lincoln Road alone had about 15 wineries. Wine had already seeped into George's blood.

Corbans had been established by the Lebanese Assid Corban in 1902, and Babich's in 1916. Then came a new crop: Selaks and I Yukich and Sons (which became Montana Wines in 1960/61) in 1934; Nobilo's in 1943; and Delegat's in 1947. In contrast to these reasonably established companies, Babich's, with its 20 acres of grapes, was considered a sizeable operation. George loved visiting the property, where the family was always so welcoming. The reception was also warm at the Delegat household — and close. Vidosava Delegat, the mother of current Delegat Wines chairman Jim Delegat, looked after the Fistonich children when Mandica was ill.

All through his late teens and early twenties, George hung around with the Babichs, particularly Joe. When he and Joe and others in their group went out for a night of socialising, a regular haunt was the Hi Diddle Griddle on Karangahape Road, where wine was served in tea cups. Another was Piccolo, at the top of Pitt Street. Auckland's handful of restaurants were run by Europeans who found New Zealand's draconian, often Kafkaesque, liquor-licensing laws — established to protect the interests of the beer industry, but also a hangover of the wowserism of the Temperance period — incredibly restrictive.

George sampling the
vintage in the winery.

But there were ways around them. George and his mates discovered that once you got to know the proprietors, and provided you were discreet, they would allow you to bring in your own wine and they would serve it in tea cups.

The more George saw how families in the wine business were progressing, the more fascinated he became by the very enterprise of winemaking and the potential for a wine industry in New Zealand — and the more determined he became to be a winemaker. George often spent time working in Frank and Elsie Yukich's vineyard and orchard, and he had observed how his sister's husband, along with his brother Mate, was developing Montana into a highly successful wine company. And it had started out so simply. Elsie had a large hen-house, built by George, so that she could have chooks and sell eggs for pin money. She also had a wine shop under the house. From small beginnings something great was growing.

In 1955 the New Zealand wine industry received another legislative boost when Parliament reduced the quantity of table wine that re-sellers could sell per sale, from two gallons (nine litres) to a quart (around a litre). This meant consumers could buy smaller quantities at a time, and this in turn meant packaging became more important. At the same time the government increased the number of re-sellers' licences, and the number of retail wine stores around the country grew. There were still strict rules in place governing where and how these licences could be awarded, and the majority of the bottled wine sold was still imported, but the sales environment was changing and local winemakers became confident that there was a living to be made from wine.

A further loosening of the regulations came in 1958, following release of a wide-ranging report by the government-appointed Winemaking Industry Committee. The committee's recommendations — that the number of import licences for wines and spirits be halved and taxes on beer and spirits be increased — had an immediate and positive effect on wine sales. This was not what the breweries wanted: for years they had argued that wine shops were unnecessary as consumers could already buy their wine from hotels.

AROUND THIS TIME Frank and Mate Yukich decided they wanted a retail outlet away from their winery on Scenic Drive. It was believed that the only licence available to them — the wine re-sellers' licence — did not permit this, and their initial application for a retail outlet in Avondale was rejected after objections from other wine sellers in the area.

At the time George's brother Ivan was working at Subritzky & Ryan, a high-profile law practice in Auckland. One Sunday at a family lunch with Frank and Elsie, the conversation turned to the Yukichs' problems with gaining their licence. Ivan mentioned that Kevin Ryan, a partner in the firm, had discovered a loophole in the legislation that could perhaps work to the Yukichs' advantage.

At this time, Ryan was becoming prominent in legal circles. Highly ambitious, he was happy to take on a case that might challenge the establishment. His contention was that, as written, anyone who put even so much as a drop of wine in a barrel could be considered a winemaker and therefore eligible for a licence. If they could show the Avondale site to be a winery, the licence could not be refused.

So, the Yukich brothers, Ivan and George Fistonich, and Kevin Ryan formed a partnership to test the law. Initially, things did not go well, but Ryan persisted, and eventually on behalf of Frank Yukich took out a writ of mandamus against the magistrate Mr Sinclair SM to issue the licence. The case was won and the shop duly opened, eventually becoming a very popular outlet for Montana Wines.

However, the application and subsequent legal case had been protracted and costly. Neither George nor Ivan had the financial wherewithal to continue their involvement, and so the partnership was dissolved, and eventually the licence was issued solely in the name of the Yukich brothers.

Despite such hiccups, if ever there was a time for a keen young man to make a move into a new industry, this was it. The laws around the making and selling of wine were being relaxed, interest in wine was growing at a rapid pace, and dining at restaurants was becoming more firmly entrenched in the Kiwi lifestyle.

But it would have to be more than a business: you had to *love* wine.

The tipping point for George Fistonich, really, was the exposure he'd had to great European table wines through his uncle George Popovic, who was a true wine connoisseur with a sophisticated lifestyle that George had strong aspirations to share.

Popovic played the stock market and was a stylish man of the times, importing Roodeberg wine from South Africa in an era when South African wine was at the height of its quality, and also buying French and German wines. When the Fistonich children had stayed at the Popovics', Uncle George had made sure his nephews and niece got to taste his wine and appreciate its qualities. He also used to take George with him to visit the Babichs whenever he was buying some of their very good dry red.

'These were all key influences that I couldn't escape and which made me want to get into the wine business,' George remembers. 'Once I had it in my mind that I wanted to make wine, there was nothing anyone could say to change my mind.'

So he went to his father, who initially could not support the decision. Andrija, who was himself buying bulk wine from Mick Erceg (father of the late Michael Erceg, who founded Independent Liquor) at Pacific Wines to blend into his own wine, thereby extending his stock, saw the stranglehold that the breweries still had on licensed premises and liquor sales outlets, and believed that smaller family vineyards would never be able to fully compete. The breweries were the competition; they were tough, they had deep pockets, and they were making it pretty hard to sell wine.

George was not persuaded — nor deterred. 'I thought he was wrong, and I put it down to his intellectual bent and the frustration he felt with life in general, with having had to work in the freezing works and gumfields.'

Frustrated by his father, George announced that he was going to buy a 60-acre farm in Clevedon, where he would run a few cows and plant his own vineyard. It was something of a hollow threat; he was only 21, and the only money he had was from buying and selling motorbikes and cars, and the occasional building work he could fit in around his apprenticeship and working alongside his parents.

However, with the help of Blair Webster, a lawyer acquaintance, he managed to scrape together a deposit, persuaded his uncle to act as guarantor for the balance, and duly purchased the property. It would come to be very useful in the future, when raising capital for other projects became difficult.

4
THE FAMILY BUSINESS

Whatever Andrija might have preferred, George's entry into the family wine business would eventuate, if not quite by planning then by sideways drift. By the early 1960s Andrija's asthma was severe. Andrija could no longer work full-time in the winery, so he agreed that George, for a start, could lease half an acre of the five-acre property and start his own winemaking business, and see if he could make something of it.

George Fistonich and
Gail Kirkpatrick at a
party not long after
they met.

T the situation was discussed with Ivan, who said he had no real interest in the winery business. With that approval, Andrija agreed that George would take a lease over the five acres on Kirkbride Road and would have the freedom to do whatever he thought was required to build up the business.

If building up the winery business was a burning goal in George's life, there was also another: wooing Gail Kirkpatrick, whom he had met in 1959 at a twenty-first party at which Gail had arrived on the arm of one of George's friends. During the course of the evening she and George were introduced. The attraction was mutual: he — good-looking, sociable and interesting; she — petite, pretty and vivacious.

Just a few days after the party, George called Gail and asked her out. Gail, interested but not yet smitten, agreed. Their first date was to a ball at the Peter Pan Cabaret, at the top of Queen Street. It was a place they would come to frequent many, many times over the course of their courtship; there, and the Point Chevalier Sailing Club, the Crystal Palace in Balmoral, and St Stephens in Khyber Pass, where they danced the night away to the big brass sound of Arthur Skelton and his band, drinking alcohol smuggled in hidden in the wraps and stoles that completed the ladies' outfits.

During an early conversation their occupations were discussed. Gail, a non-Catholic, told George she was working as a secretary at Charles Haines Advertising, where Ray Dalton, father of the legendary All-Black-to-be, Andy Dalton, was her boss. George's description of his job was a little more intriguing. 'I asked him what he did,' Gail remembers. 'He told me he had just come out of his apprenticeship and was now going to make wine. Well, that concept was totally foreign to me. I knew what wine was, but it wasn't something I knew much more about, and I had no idea how it was made. But I thought, well, okay — that makes him even more interesting.'

Gail began spending time at the Fistonich property in Mangere, where she could see the tension between George and his father. 'George got along reasonably well with his mother, but around the time we met he was becoming a little frustrated with his father, who was, like many of the Croatians I have met, a strong-willed individual. Mostly it was about what was happening around the winery, but it was also about what George was doing with any spare time he had. His parents thought he should be working at the winery all the hours available, and what George, who was quite social, really wanted was to go out on a Friday and Saturday night just as his friends did — I mean, that's what happened in those days. Friday and Saturday were for going out, not working around the home washing bottles or pressing grapes. It seemed that, in spite of having lived in New Zealand all those years, they had retained their very traditional Croatian sense of what family commitment meant, and perhaps found it difficult to accept their children going out and enjoying themselves.'

George and Gail's courtship lasted 18 months, interrupted for a couple of months by Gail's decision to travel with a friend to the South Island, where they found work at the Hermitage Hotel. On her return, it became clear that George's intentions were more serious than Gail had thought. 'I realised he was really keen. I mean, I was living at home with my parents in Devonport, so he had to come all the way from Mangere if he wanted to see me.'

Gail's father was an accomplished photographer, who at the time owned a dairy in Browns Bay further up the North Shore. George's charm worked on Gail's parents as well as it had worked on her, and, after some early reservations about the vast difference in their backgrounds, they grew to think very highly of him. Eventually George went to Gail's father to ask for permission to propose to his daughter. He gave his blessing, and the couple were married on 1 November 1961 at St Francis de Sales Catholic Church in Devonport.

The honeymoon was in Taupo, and on their return George and Gail moved into a small house in Cornwall Road, Mangere East, that George and his brother Ivan had bought and renovated as an investment. It was the first of many properties the couple would own, and the first time either of them had moved out of their parents' homes. But the independence of having their own home wasn't to last.

GEORGE STARTED OFF part-time at the winery, as he didn't have the money to work there full-time or to buy the equipment he knew he needed. To keep the cash flow coming, he kept on with some building work for his relatives, and carried on buying and selling the odd car and motorbike that he would pick up cheaply at auctions.

At first he continued making the port and sherry his father had made. Then he started making a dry white (Hock) and a dry red. (The terminology 'Hock' was European — after the German Rhineland white wine Hochheimer — and it was common during this period for New Zealand wines to be given European names, a practice that later became illegal.) George sold pretty much everything he made from the house, but occasionally, mostly at night, he would approach one or two restaurants that he knew wanted wine to serve their guests, which at the time was still illegal. Soon he became adept at getting them to take wine, but never in very great quantities.

Then one day he saw a newspaper advertisement for barrels and filters that were for sale at Maungatapu Vineyard, just outside Tauranga. The vineyard was owned by a now little-known wine pioneer, the distinguished World War One RAF pilot Air Commodore Francis Hewlett, who in 1939 had begun making Müller Thurgau and Riesling. He returned to air force duties during World War Two as the commander of the Ohakea and Hobsonville bases for the RNZAF. After

CLARET

DRY RED TABLE WINE

MANUFACTURED AND BOTTLED AT THE CELLARS OF

VILLA MARIA WINES LTD.

3 KIRKBRIDE ROAD, MANGERE, AUCKLAND

One of George's early
labels.

the war he continued making wine, but he found the wet Tauranga climate very challenging and the market for wines frustratingly slow to develop. Eventually, he had decided to get rid of everything. Hewlett had about 20 barrels, ranging in size from 1500 litres to 3500 litres and made mostly of totara. Lack of use had caused the wood to dry out, and the barrels were falling apart. He also had a filter and a couple of pumps and some laboratory equipment.

Hewlett was impressed by the enthusiasm and confidence of the young Fistonich, and agreed to sell him the lot for £3000. This was a lot of money given how little George was taking from the vineyard each week, but he came up with a deposit and Hewlett gave him three years to pay off the rest. He tossed in an old 1930 Chevy truck as part of the deal.

George had an old four-tonne truck that he had bought for £90 at Government Auctions, and he made 10 trips down to Tauranga with a couple of mates, Ivan Posa and Joe Shine, and, occasionally, Gail, to bring all the equipment up to Mangere, wrapped string around the barrels to hold them together.

'My father thought I was completely stark-staring mad. He told me I wouldn't be able to do anything with the barrels. My mother was more quietly supportive. We put them on the lawn, and turned the garden sprinklers on them for about a week. As they swelled up, we tightened them up. A little of the carpentry skill I had learned came in handy.'

In the first few months Andrija helped out by looking after the customers. Mandica assisted, too, and Gail would come and help out in the shop. Apart from that, George was pretty much on his own. As he worked in the vines, pruning and hand-weeding, there was plenty of time for hatching big plans. He and Joe Babich had launched a Young Winemakers Club, of which Ivan Selak, Nick Nobilo, Jim Delegat and others interested in the potential of table wines were members.

George also continued to work part-time with his brother-in-law Frank Yukich, who was in the process of a major expansion of Montana Wines, then based on Scenic Drive, just out of Titirangi. Although they got on well socially, the working relationship between Frank and George, who were both strong-minded, was sometimes tense. 'Frank and George worked night and day,' remembers Gail Fistonich. They were building a wine shop in Tokoroa and there was some kind of argument. At that point George decided to put his foot down and say enough is enough.'

George recalls the argument well, because it involved Gail. 'Frank had gained a licence to open a retail outlet in Tokoroa. He needed to tidy up the shop and install some shelves, so I went with him to help. We stayed in town for about three weeks while this was going on, working long hours from early in the morning to late at night, then going to parties most nights. Anyway, one Thursday he told me that we were going to a party in Whakatane the next night. I told him I wanted to go to Auckland to see Gail for the weekend and would rather work the Friday so I could get away on the Saturday morning. He wasn't pleased and implied I was taking too much time off, and more or less told me I couldn't go. I wasn't having anyone stopping me from going to Auckland, so I just went anyway. While I was away I decided it was time to focus on my own dream of making wine.'

IT WAS A MILESTONE in September 1961 when George decided to register Villa Maria Wines. It was a marketing and positioning move, one of the early signs of how deeply he was thinking about the business and where it might take him. 'Montana already had this mountain theme, and I wanted to distinguish myself from them. I also thought Villa Maria had a more international ring to it,' he explains. 'The New Zealand wine industry had a bad name — mostly for making poor-quality hybrid wine — and I was not interested in being involved at that low level. I was already thinking about the export market as early as 1961, although I don't quite know why, because at that stage we were not making a lot of wine and there was no way I had the resources to be selling it overseas.'

Nonetheless, he decided to start as he meant to go on. 'I asked Batley Printing Company to make me up a letterhead. I was quite pleased really, because it looked quite impressive. I was very fussy and particular about things like that.'

He was a young, newly married man with big plans and growing ambition, and he and his mates would chat about their goals and their ideas. They would meet at the trendy Quintet Café near John Courts on the corner of Victoria and Queen streets, which was accessed by stairs down to a basement. It served what then passed for good coffee, and was frequented by advertising agency and law practice people. George may have been a hardworking immigrant's son from Mangere Bridge, but he had sophisticated and aspirational tastes. He moved in a circle of young people who saw the future as full of promise. It was the 1960s, and buttoned-down New Zealand was loosening up a little: there was fun and enterprise to be had.

George was ever restless, ever moving forward. He would be the one in the group who wanted to discuss things and toss plans and ideas around. Some may have seen him as ambitious, although he never considered himself to be. Rather he'd describe himself as organised, and fussy about quality and long-term potential, with an overall impatience to make things happen.

In 1960 there had been a further relaxation of the liquor-licensing laws when for the first time the government legislated to allow restaurants to sell wine. With that law change, the state of the New Zealand dining environment and the wine industry would change forever. George had picked just the right moment to become a winemaker.

Early advertisements.

5
SUCCESSION

*In May 1962 Andrija had
a serious bout of asthma,
and he was driving himself to the
local doctor's for an adrenaline
injection when he had an
unexpected heart attack. He died
in the doctor's surgery. He and
Mandica were just weeks away
from moving into their new house
on the top corner of the vineyard
in Creamery Road. Elsie had just
had her fifth child and could be
of little help, and Gail was also
expecting her first child.*

Mandica and Andrija Fistonich,
not long before Andrija's
sudden death.

I t was a tough time for the family. 'We got through it, but it was hard work,' George remembers. 'Gail, who had already been thrown into the deep end of another culture with many expectations of her, was wonderful.'

Gail, a North Shore girl, had already experienced how different it was to be a woman in the chauvinistic Croatian community. 'The older generation of Croatian women were very strong and hardworking but seldom admitted to being really well,' Gail says. 'They almost competed with each other to see who was the hardest worker. It was the same for Mandica, however she did have some ill health. When she took to her bed, I, as the daughter-in-law, was expected to fulfil the role of caregiver to both her and Andrija. One time just after we were first married, Mandica was convalescing at her sister's place in Avóndale after a brief illness. I was at Kirkbride Road cooking for George and his father. Andrija would get on the phone to his wife. It would seem to me that he was yelling, but he always spoke like that — in fact many of the older Croatians seemed to speak very loudly and quickly on the phone, as if that was the only way they could be heard at the other end. If they were speaking Croatian, it sounded to me as though they were arguing. I would ask, what on earth are you arguing about? But of course it was just the very animated way they spoke to each other.'

She would be struck by this chauvinism years later, when in 2001 George and Gail travelled to Croatia on holiday with their old friends

Ross (founder of Matua Valley Wines) and Adrienne Spence. While there, they met George's cousin, whom he had not previously met. Gail remembers that the cousin and his wife lived in a 'very humble little cottage on what seemed like barren land, with no stove or anything that looked like you could cook on it'.

There was a large fish on the table, and Adrienne and Gail discussed where and how the fish would be cooked. 'George's cousin sat at the end of the table and did not lift a finger, not a finger. His wife disappeared, and then eventually the cousin asked if we wanted to watch Katica cook the fish. We went outside, and there was a small stone shed behind the house and poor Katica was down on her hands and knees inside, perspiration pouring out of her, hunched over the fire cooking the fish and the eggplant. When she came inside, she didn't sit down but kept serving us. I would look over at George, who was looking a bit embarrassed, and I thought, now I know what it's all about. Now I know what the relationship between the Croatian men and their wives means.'

There were two rooms in the house, and in one, 'the front bedroom', lived George's aunt. 'Apparently the rumour was that something had upset her about 10 years before, and she had put herself to bed and not got up since,' Gail remembers. 'She had a whistle and she would lie in bed and whistle for Katica, who would have to run and fetch for her. She would not eat what they were eating, and had to have everything ground up before she would eat it. This was the daughter-in-law's life in old Croatia.'

George's most vivid memory of the visit involved almonds and figs. 'Katica had put a couple of bowls of freshly harvested almonds and figs on the table and Ross and I ate them. My cousin noticed they were all gone and asked if we wanted more. We said yes, and he disappeared outside and came back with another couple of bowls. Katica walked in, saw the bowls, and said, "Cousin George, I have been married to this man for over 30 years and this is the first time he has ever picked fruit to put on the table." I said to Ross, maybe we should leave Gail and Adrienne here for training.'

Andrija's death highlighted the cultural differences that would

The Mangere property on
the corner of Creamery
and Kirkbride roads,
showing the concrete
tanks that held the wine
before the advent of
stainless steel.

come to colour Gail's perception of the lives of Croatian women. 'I was thrown into it — boy, was this Kiwi girl thrown right into it. At the funeral, George's mother and all the aunts and cousins were weeping and wailing, which was the traditional way in the 1960s and 1970s, and I was thrust into the kitchen and made responsible for making sure everyone was fed and kept happy, etc. I knew I was being watched to see how I would handle everything. It was something that seemed to happen a lot during those first years.'

When shortly afterwards George told Gail they would be moving into the family home in Kirkbride Road with Mandica, she wasn't sure it would work out. 'It was incredibly stressful. When Andrija died, he and Mandica had been in the process of building a house up the road. It had been designed by George's brother Ivan, but it wasn't finished and so she had to stay where she was. She stayed in mourning for months, and as with many Croatian women, mourning was expected to continue and be shared. There was no escaping her grief, and sometimes I wondered what I had got myself into.'

Eventually Mandica, who still liked to dabble in the winemaking, moved into her new home on the property. Life seemed set to become a little more settled. However, Mandica was still a force in their lives. On one occasion one of the workers at Villa told George that he believed Mandica was operating a still in her home. When George next went to see his mother, he discovered in her basement a fully operational still, complete with copper pipes and winemaking equipment. She was still making her precious rakija. George had to tell her that what she was doing was illegal, and that if she was discovered it could reflect badly on him. He insisted it had to go, and Mandica's life as a winemaker and illegal spirit-maker finally came to an end.

WITH ANDRIJA GONE, the vineyard was now very firmly George's responsibility. But things were looking tough. There was plenty of negativity about what he was doing, and it came from various quarters. 'We used to sell most of our wine out of the room that served as a shop at the front of the house. We had regular customers, mostly local, who would come in and look for their sweet sherry and the port that my father had made. The market in those days was 95 per cent sweet port and sweet sherry,' George remembers. 'I would offer them a taste of the dry red or dry white I was making, and they used to say it tasted like vinegar and they wanted their sweet port and sweet sherry. Many of them would be disgusted.

'Ivan would bring his fellow law students back home, and they would tell me that a typical Kiwi was unsophisticated and would not know his dry white from his dry red. They would say, "And what the hell are you making this for? Who is going to buy it apart from us?" And they did have a point, but I passionately debated the point with them. I sort of semi-forced people to take it and experiment with food as it was good for their health. Looking back now, many of them must have thought I was a nutcase!'

This was an era when sales of fortified wines were at their peak, and Villa Maria would become a leader in the market sector. George, however, was convinced that good-quality generic table wines were the future of the industry, and he produced a Villa Maria Hock and a Burgundy, with some considerable consumer success. To supplement the meagre supply of grapes from the Kirkbride Road vineyard, George would travel to the vineyards of Henderson and Kumeu and as far south as Te Kauwhata to purchase as many grapes as he could find.

These trips were not without their own drama, as future employee Ross Spence recalls. 'The three Cossiboom brothers — Max, Gordon and Lenny — were bloody hard-case. Max was actually quite intelligent, Gordon was quieter, but Lenny was a real rough bastard. These three guys just loved George, and used to help him out on weekends and at nights, particularly during harvest, picking grapes, clearing up and just general labour. At some stage Lenny began driving George's big old Fordson truck down to Te Kauwhata to collect a load of grapes to bring back up to Villa. On one trip the truck got a puncture. They put the tyre-jack under the truck, but the guys had loaded the truck so heavy that it just pushed the jack and the boards underneath it into the ground. So Lenny pushed a lot of the grapes out of the truck

VILLA MARIA

MANUFACTURED & BOTTLED AT THE CELLARS OF
VILLA MARIA WINES LTD.
3 KIRKBRIDE ROAD, MANGERE, AUCKLAND

VILLA MARIA

ESTATE BOTTLED

Hock

DRY WHITE TABLE WINE

PRODUCED AND BOTTLED AT THE CELLARS OF
VILLA MARIA WINES LTD.
5 KIRKBRIDE RD. MANGERE, AUCKLAND, NEW ZEALAND

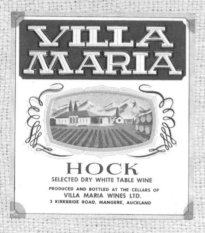

VILLA MARIA

HOCK

SELECTED DRY WHITE TABLE WINE

PRODUCED AND BOTTLED AT THE CELLARS OF
VILLA MARIA WINES LTD.
3 KIRKBRIDE ROAD, MANGERE, AUCKLAND

VILLA MARIA

FINEST   QUALITY

PRODUCT OF NEW ZEALAND

GOLDEN SHERRY

PRODUCED & BOTTLED AT THE CELLARS OF
VILLA MARIA WINES LTD.
3 KIRKBRIDE ROAD, MANGERE, AUCKLAND

VILLA MARIA

ESTATE BOTTLED

Rosé

A DELICATE SEMI-DRY TABLE WINE

PRODUCED AND BOTTLED AT THE CELLARS OF
VILLA MARIA WINES LTD.
5 KIRKBRIDE RD. MANGERE, AUCKLAND, NEW ZEALAND

Villa Maria Estate

Dry White '74

A Dry White Table Wine • Chill Before Serving

VILLA MARIA WINES LTD. KIRKBRIDE RD, MANGERE AUCKLAND, N.Z.
CONTENTS 750ml ALC. CONT. 11.5% BY VOL. APPROX.

**MOUNTAIN VALLEY
DRY WHITE
1980**

*A mouth tingling dry white
wine suitable for any
occasion.*

Serve chilled

VILLA MARIA

Made and bottled on   the Villa Maria Estate

CONTENTS 2250ml. ALCOHOL CONTENT 10.5% BY VOLUME

A PRODUCT OF VILLA MARIA WINES LTD. AUCKLAND NEW ZEALAND

Special Cuvée

750ml.
Vinted and bottled
by
Villa Maria Wines Ltd. Auckland
Alc. cont. 11.5% by vol. approx.

Villa Maria Estate

Traminer

A selected dry white wine
made from the highly
flavoured-perfumed
gerwurtztraminer grape.
Store lying down.
Serve chilled.

1977

750ml
Alc. cont. 10.5% by vol. approx

VILLA MARIA WINES LTD
Kirkbridge Road, Mangere,
Auckland, New Zealand.

VILLA MARIA

SANGRIA

The evolving design of
Villa Maria label, from the
1960s to the early 1980s.

onto the side of the road, changed the tyre and then shovelled the grapes back onto the truck before continuing the drive back to the winery. On another occasion, the truck's water system failed and the truck caught fire on the Mangere bridge — Lenny just took off and left it for someone else to go and sort out. George really relied on this truck and would do anything to keep it operating. One day I arrived to find George cracking a dozen eggs into the radiator to seal the holes that had appeared on a trip back from Te Kauwhata. It worked! It was really Kiwi number-eight wire stuff in those days. It may have been his first attempt at innovation,' George laughs.

In 1963 Villa Maria entered its wine into competitions for the first time. The two 1962 vintage dry reds — a Burgundy and a Claret (the early New Zealand wine industry was still using traditional wine nomenclature) made from Henderson Valley fruit — were entered in the Royal Easter Show and got second and third prize. Villa Maria and George Fistonich were suddenly on the map. There was no dissuading George from his chosen path, and the awards were the spur he needed to press on. But it wouldn't be easy.

GAIL HAD GIVEN BIRTH to their first child, Karen, about a month after Andrija's death. As soon as she was able, Gail took over the wine sales at the winery so George could go out selling during the day and work at night. In 1963, just 11 months later, Michael was born, and then three-and-a-half years later, in 1966, Megan arrived. But having three very young children did not excuse Gail from contributing to the other work around the property, including looking after visitors. 'Friends and relatives would be brought in to lend a hand at critical times, such as harvest and bottling. They used our laundry to wash the bottles, and they would always be in and out of the house. I would go out and help pick grapes, then I would have to rush in and prepare food for the helpers.'

Then there were the customers. 'We had a lean-to on the side of the house. People would arrive at all times of night and day and would push a bell, and I would have to drop the babies and rush out to serve these old girls who came for their jar of sherry. Inevitably they would want to spend half an hour or longer sipping the little glass of free wine we would give them. Meanwhile I was thinking, I wonder what the kids are doing?'

They were extremely hard-up, but occasionally there was some relief. Local farmer and family friend Brian Ogilvy would come and work in the wine shop, freeing up Gail to do the grocery shopping. 'I would ask George for money from the till and he would say, how much do you need? It wasn't much in those days — I suppose probably around £3 — but we could get by on that then.'

With George fully committed at the winery, and with three young children, there was little opportunity for socialising after-hours, but the constant stream of visitors to Kirkbride Road ensured that life was never dull. Through those years they saw a lot of George's cousin Tony Babich (the son of Andrija's sister and her husband, who had a winery next door before moving away to Mangere Bridge) and his wife Maria, who were a similar age.

They saw something of George's brother Ivan, who would later marry Betty Radich, a granddaughter of the Lavas family who had taken in George's father when he first came to New Zealand, but more of Peter Popovic, George's younger brother. For a time Peter worked for George, with the aim of buying into the business with money he inherited. But he also had a bent for nightclubs, and after three years decided he wanted to buy into the Cordova Reception Lounge in Mangere. Later he went into partnership with Warwick Wright in Oliver's Changing Times, a glamorous (for the times) Fort Street nightclub. He then went to work in marketing with a juice company owned by Coca Cola Bottlers before leaving to form his own juice company. This company experienced financial difficulties, and he subsequently joined the educational book publisher Wendy Pye. After a short period he left to live in Australia, where he died, aged only 54, in 2001.

'We haven't got a good record of a long-living family,' George says of his brothers' and father's early deaths. 'Elsie and I have to live long to beat the odds.'

LEFT

George and Michael at
the winery with Caesar
the watch-dog. In the
background are the
early concrete tanks.

ABOVE

George and Gail at an
industry dinner.

In those early years, and throughout their marriage, there has been a distinct, if unspoken, acceptance of the different roles George and Gail would each play both within the business and in regard to the family. 'George was involved in raising the children and was very much a part of their lives, but I wouldn't say it was on a day-to-day basis,' says Gail. 'He was in the business, and it was my job to make sure the house ran smoothly. We didn't discuss things in those terms, it's just the way things worked out.'

When circumstances required George to take a more active role, his response was sometimes a little unpredictable. When Karen turned five she was sent to Our Lady of the Sacred Heart in Epsom. A year later, Michael followed. In 1969, when Megan was three, Gail had to have an operation, leaving George to look after the children.

'George picked me up from the hospital and brought me home, and I had to go straight to bed. Then he came in and said, "There is something I have to tell you." Michael must have been five or six at the time, and had come home and said, "Dad, our teacher is going to give us a talk on Spain and wants me to bring in one or two bottles of wine tomorrow so that all the kids in the class can have a little taste." So the next morning, George gave Michael a bottle or two of wine to take to school. I am listening to this story and all I could see was this little child going up to the teacher with his bottles of wine.

'She sat the wine on the desk, and then the headmaster walked in and asked her, "What's this wine doing here?" She told him of her plans to give the children a "wee taste" as part of this talk on Spain. Next thing the headmaster is telephoning George and saying, "Mr Fistonich, I want to thank you very much for sending the wine, but I am very sorry but the children can't taste it — it's not appropriate." I was thinking, of all the times for something like this to happen! But of course George, always the wine promoter, doesn't think like me. He wouldn't think of the consequences, or if there might be anything unusual about a five-year-old taking wine to school, or a teacher giving children a taste, or of how it might appear to an outsider looking in.'

6
THINKING BIGGER

In the mid-1960s, New Zealand wine drinkers, while small in number, were beginning to get a taste for the local product. Before then, restrictive legislation had forced wine drinkers to choose from a limited range of poorer-quality imports from France and Germany. And knowledge of different wines and vintages was scant. George knew that getting people to taste his wines was key to their developing an appreciation for them, so he embarked on his own minor crusade to place wine and food in the same environment.

IT'S A MATTER OF TASTE

Deciding on all the liquor requirements was made so much easier when Pauline and Baden called on Villa Maria Wines.

Villa Maria's friendly experts were soon able to discuss and offer the couple the type of wines they were after.

Baden and Pauline say they have no hesitation at all in recommending Villa Maria Wines to any couple intending to get married.

VILLA MARIA WINES
3 KIRKBRIDE ROAD, MANGERE
PHONE 669-207

George began to offer community groups and customers the opportunity to participate in wine-and-cheese evenings, where tasting-glasses of Villa Maria wine were served with pieces of cheese, and George or one of his staff would give a brief talk about the wine. These events were promoted under the general slogan of 'Let Villa Maria introduce you to wine' and proved to be very popular. The campaign even had its own song recorded by 1960s Kiwi rock legend Tommy Adderley, and was played frequently on pirate radio station Radio Hauraki.

As Keith Stewart writes in *Chancers and Visionaries — A History of Wine in New Zealand*, 'after one of these events most attendees were on first name terms with Hock and Moselle perhaps even Pinotage and Champagne . . . In a nation where small talk was traditionally restricted to rugby, racing and the neighbours, this was indeed a radical development.'

George was unstoppable in pursuit of sales. Indeed, on their honeymoon Gail was mightily unimpressed when he stopped to deliver wine to a Tokoroa wine shop on their way to Taupo. In the early years of Villa Maria, George would load cases of wine into his car and cold-call stores and restaurants, something he would continue to do until 1969. His travels took him to wine retailers all over the North Island — from the Bay of Islands, Whangarei and Wellsford in the north, to Tokoroa, Hamilton, Te Awamutu, Rotorua, Opotiki, Tauranga,

Katikati and Te Puke in the south . . . anywhere and everywhere he could find a liquor store.

These trips often meant time away from Kirkbride Road and the family, but they were essential in building up his credibility with independent retailers, something that would work to his great advantage in years to come.

His very first retailer in Wellington was Mike Aspros, who had a famous wine shop in Wakefield Street called John Bull Wines. A lively character, Aspros would regularly come up to Auckland to visit wineries and buy stock, and he became Fistonich's first agent in Wellington.

IN 1969 GEORGE decided to build a new 12,000-square-foot winery. He had an architect draw up the plans and borrowed around $30,000 from the bank to pay for it. It was an enormously stressful time: not only did he have this major loan, but he had also borrowed money to buy a house in Epsom.

The last vintage made in the original winery was in 1969; Villa Maria moved into the new winery in time for the 1970 vintage. George was eager to ensure that his winery was as impressive as he could make it, and he hired a landscape gardener who planted pohutukawa trees and beautiful gardens along the winery frontage on Kirkbride Road. He employed full-time staff, including Gail's sister Anne Iremonger, for the first time.

It was around this time that George employed Gail Harding as his secretary-cum-Girl Friday. He credits Gail with being an essential and important part of the early team. 'Gail really ran the show. Not only was she my PA, she was also the credit controller and the accountant, and she kept everyone under her thumb, making sure they kept up with any paperwork, filed their expenses correctly, and followed up on any phone orders. I don't know how I would have managed without her at the time.'

Those first years were in many ways a family affair: Gail's husband, Ted Harding, and other couples would run wine-and-cheese evenings at social events all over the city as part of the early drive to

New stainless steel tanks
being installed at the winery.
The old concrete tanks stand
alongside the winery building.

VILLA MARIA

Melesconera

1970

A vinifera-hybrid, Melesconera is grown extensively in the Loire district of France. It was imported into New Zealand by the Government Research Station at Te Kauwhata in 1936. A medium to heavy bearer, it produces a soft, delicate, dry red wine tending towards a Rose but entirely vinifera in character with a pleasant astringency. Ideal with salads and light red meats.
Serve slightly below room temperature.   Store lying down.
Bin 1/70.

PRODUCED AND BOTTLED AT THE CELLARS OF

VILLA MARIA WINES LTD.

5 KIRKBRIDE RD, MANGERE, AUCKLAND, NEW ZEALAND

George was experimenting with new varietals very early on.

The indispensable
Kevin Blincoe, one
of George's first
winery employees,
hand-loading apple
boxes of grapes
into the first of the
new-era crushers.

BELOW

The cellar door
entrance of the
Kirkbride Road winery.

get consumers tasting wine. 'We had no real cool storage, so we kept stocks of wine in about seven different fridges upstairs at the winery. Ted, and other married couples looking for part-time work, would take what he needed and go out and run these parties, which actually turned out to be quite successful in getting our name known.'

Another early and key employee was Kevin Blincoe, Villa's first operations manager. Blincoe was to remain with George for more than 14 years. 'He and my foreman at the time, Michael McCullough, were a great team whom I came to rely on hugely.'

The new winery was a considerable operation for the time, and included stainless-steel tanks. Before that, most of the wine had been made in concrete tanks. The new winery was a major step up. George was no longer a one-man-band, but someone running a more complex business with heavier financial commitments. There was now a need for serious sales objectives.

BUT PERHAPS IT WAS George's decision to offer a job to Ross Spence — one of a raft of people to have worked with George at Villa Maria and then gone on to have a stellar career in the New Zealand wine industry — that was his first real stroke of genius. 'I met Ross through David Betts of Betts Engineering, started by David's father, suppliers of filling machines and equipment to the wine industry,' remembers George. 'Betts and Ross were very close friends, and at a party we were both at we got talking about wine. At the time Ross was driving bulldozers for Hooky Anderson, which seemed a little odd to me. Ross had been enrolled in a degree in viticulture at Fresno University in California and had a very good knowledge of grape-growing and a passion for grape varieties. My understanding is that when he came home he wanted to do his own thing and was working towards creating his own vineyard. Up until this stage I had been pretty much doing everything myself, with a little help from family and friends. Things were going reasonably well, but I was pushed to the limit. I felt that Ross's education was being wasted, so I said to him, "Do you want to work for me?"' Spence's arrival at Villa Maria was to give George the push into growth and into winning the respect from the industry.

One of the first things George handed Ross Spence when he arrived at the winery was a spade. George had recently bought 10 acres of market-garden land right next door, and he and Spence planted the new block with Palomino and Pinotage grapes themselves. In addition they planted Seibel 4643 and 5455 and Barco 22A, which would give George many more options for expanding his portfolio. In one hit, the new planting would take Villa Maria from a five-acre property to a 15-acre property with serious volume potential. This sort of scale made George's ambitions for a viable business suddenly look achievable.

Spence became the official winemaker in 1971, freeing up George to attend to other parts of the business. It was a happy partnership. 'He was incredibly bright and a very good winemaker,' George says of Spence. 'He had quite an academic approach. He was quite structured in his approach, probably because of his university education. He was very much into budgets and planning and the need to put everything on paper. Spence also had a great passion for viticulture. And he used this passion for the industry's benefit when he became a director, and subsequently chairman, of New Zealand Winemakers. He's made an outstanding contribution. He lives and breathes the wine industry, and has always been very involved in promoting its best interests, particularly improving the overall standards of New Zealand wine producers and ensuring they have a truly international perspective that works in our favour. He has been a great friend of Villa Maria, and he and his wife Adrienne have been close personal friends to Gail and me over the years.'

Another Spence — Ross's brother, Bill — came along around 1972, working on and off for Villa Maria for almost three years in operations and dispatch.

Ross Spence's passion for viticulture was well-known, and George knew that he was keen to go out to do his own thing. It was all in the open, there was no secret about its inevitability. The question was simply of when he might go. 'In fact, Ross used to ask me about budgets and things like that,' George remembers. 'When Ross and Bill

At first George did not have
the budget to build a barrel
hall and the casks of wine were
stored outside, using sheets of
iron and tarpaulins to cover
them in summer.

told me that Ross had planted his own vineyard in Waimauku I was not surprised, and in the beginning I bought most of their grapes.'

Later the brothers informed George that they were going to set up their own small winery, called Matua Valley, after the road Ross lived on in Huapai. They started making wine part-time in a tin shed in Swanson in West Auckland, and then at the end of 1973 Ross left Villa Maria to work on Matua full-time. It was a pattern that was to be repeated many times across the New Zealand wine industry since the 1970s, as keen younger people moved on to create their own businesses, taking what they had learned from mentor bosses and using it to express the *terroir* of their vineyard land and their own dreams of great wine. The connections are like a family tree, and it is that pattern and that connectivity that has driven the New Zealand wine industry forward.

Ross Spence's time in the vineyards of California had convinced him that the New Zealand *terroir* was perfectly capable of growing a range of grape varieties well beyond the limited scope of what was then currently in favour. To this end he experimented with anything he could get his hands on, including cuttings of Syrah, Sémillon, Gewürztraminer, Müller Thurgau, Pinot Noir, Flora and Sauvignon Blanc; the last, a grape George had himself been interested in early on, but had had no access to. Spence's forage through a Ministry of Agriculture facility in West Auckland had produced some unidentified vine samples with which the Spence brothers would establish their reputations as the first winemakers to introduce Sauvignon Blanc to New Zealand.

In 1973, with a tiny quantity of grapes, Ross Spence made a laboratory lot of Sauvignon Blanc at Villa Maria. Then, in 1974, the first commercial vintage of Sauvignon Blanc made by the Spence brothers came to the notice of Wayne Thomas, then the viticulturist at Montana, who thought the grape might be suitable for more extensive planting on the company's land in Marlborough. Further research took place and, after a highly favourable report from an American viticulture expert, Thomas convinced Montana owner Frank Yukich to plant large tracts of the Marlborough estate in Sauvignon Blanc. In 1979 Montana made its first Marlborough Sauvignon Blanc, now the most internationally recognisable New Zealand wine commodity.

WITH SPENCE in the winery, George could turn his attention to giving full support to his growing sales team. And just as he had struck gold with Spence, so also in Maurice Servantie had he secured a sales team leader who could work with him to drive the new business forward. Servantie's skill at developing strong and positive customer relationships was to become critical to Villa Maria's early success, so much so that George describes him as 'the most unique salesman we have ever had, with an amazing capacity to cover all of New Zealand'.

Maurie Servantie was a Brit, a former policeman, who had come out from the United Kingdom in 1962 and landed a job in Auckland with the packaging giant 3M, which was then based in Penrose. He started work the same day as another colleague, and when they discovered that they both lived on the North Shore they decided that car-pooling, using each other's car on alternate weeks, seemed the smart thing to do.

One afternoon not long after they had begun to commute across the isthmus together, Servantie's colleague said he was planning to visit a winery in Mangere on the weekend and invited Servantie to come along. And that is how he came to meet George Fistonich. George was at the winery and invited Maurie and his companion to try his wines. Over those first glasses, a long-standing friendship began. George, often short of cash, was not beyond enlisting the support of family and friends to lend a hand when there was work to be done. In exchange were wine and great barbecues. So it was that well before he became a Villa Maria employee Servantie got involved with the company.

'On one of our visits, George asked if we were doing anything one night the following week. He then told us he needed a team of five or six people to help him bottle some wine, and invited us to come and help. We duly turned up at around 5.30pm and were offered drinks.

WINE — CHEESE — BISCUITS — TOOTHPICKS — NAPKINS — GLASSES — PLATES — CARDS

YOUR CHEESE AND WINE PARTY CAN BE 'IN'

—with just a little planning

BY STAFF WRITER HEATHER STUART

CHEESE and wine parties are "in." Why? Because they're novel, sophisticated and above all, a simple way of entertaining.

They're ideal for large business get-togethers, and club parties, and they also make a welcome change from routine beer-swilling parties in private homes.

Another advantage . . . you don't have to hold them on Saturday nights at 8 p.m. Weekday cheese and wine parties, usually for business gatherings, can be held at any afternoon hour. Those holding a private party often prefer Friday or Saturday at 5 p.m. There are others, being a little different, who hold their parties on Sunday afternoon, beginning at three o'clock. It's all up to you.

Basically, these are the items you will need:

WINE
CHEESE
BISCUITS
TOOTHPICKS
NAPKINS
GLASSES
PLATES
CARDS TO IDENTIFY CHEESE AND WINES.

Before you can begin ordering the cheese and wine you will need to work out guest numbers. As a guide to wine quantities, Mr George Fistonich, an Auckland vintner suggests three-quarters of a bottle of wine for each guest.

He recommends guests should be offered a choice of:

Two dry white wines.

Two sweet white wines.

Two dry red wines.

Two medium red wines.

Two sweet red wines (the rose type).

Two madeiras.

Two sherries, dry and sweet and Two ports (only if there are older people present).

Add a few bottles of sparkling wine to the list, for there's no doubt that "popping" corks give a party an additional lift.

As a talking point, the host should aim at providing wines from different vineyards.

A bottle of New Zealand table wine will cost a little under or over 80c.

If at any time you are not sure what wines to buy, don't hesitate to consult your local wine merchant or, if you live near vineyards, the wine grower. They will always be willing to advise you.

To keep people circulating, it's a good idea to group wines of the same variety at different points of the room. This means that once guests have tasted one wine, they move off to sample another.

Arrange glasses nearby. At least two glasses for each person should be provided and always have a dozen extra to allow for mishaps. Glasses can be hired from catering firms, but prices vary, so it is as well to make inquiries.

There is no need to provide any other liquid refreshment. You will not only confuse your guests' palates but defeat the whole purpose of the party if you include gin, whisky or beer.

Although many do not realize it, the main reason for having cheese with wine is because cheese acts as a foil for wine tasting. It is necessary to clear the palate with cheese between each wine tasting, otherwise the feel of one wine will cancel out the other.

Cheese also helps absorb wines in your system.

At official wine tasting functions judges prefer a bland cheese, the dryer the better. Too strong a cheese overpowers the flavour of the wine.

There is no strict ruling as to the type of cheese you have with each wine. It's entirely your own

Set out your party table in an attractive way.

choice. More often than not, a person tries out several varieties, finds one he particularly likes and keeps to it.

But, generally, light-flavoured cheeses are associated with light wines and cheese with a dominating flavour go with robust red wines.

Mr David Corban, of Auckland, makes these suggestions for pairing wines and cheeses.

"Mild cheeses such as (mild) cheddar, colby, danbo, young gruyere and gouda go well with white wines, such as Riesling dry white, Pinot and Sauterne.

"Medium tasty cheeses such as mellow cheddar, havarti, elder gruyere, cheshire and fetta will partner clarets, dry red table wines, and dry sherries.

"A blue vein cheese goes with dry red table wine or a full-bodied rich port.

"Any type of cheese with sparkling wines."

You should allow 10c of cheese per person. Cheese should be cut into small cubes — larger pieces would too readily curb guests' appetites.

For 50 guests, Mrs Jean Leaf, of the NZ Dairy Board, recommends:

1lb mild cheddar	½lb Fetta
1lb mature cheddar	½lb Danbo
½lb smoked cheese	½lb Gouda
½lb Erbo	½lb Havarti
½lb Gruyere	½lb Blue Vein

Most people prefer a cheddar-type mild cheese . . . 80 per cent of cheese consumption in this country is of this kind. Some hosts may feel that, because of this, they should provide more mild cheese than anything else. But, as the purpose of the party is to taste, guests should be encouraged to try other varieties.

Cheese dips are always popular. Handy to these dishes leave some plain cracker biscuits and some potato chips for "dunking." Near the plates of cheese pieces have cracker biscuits (no butter) and bowls of toothpicks.

Try to buy your cheeses on the day of the party, so that they are

Please turn to Page 78

A magazine feature
on wine and cheese
— the 'in' thing!

Shortly after, Gail appeared to see how many she had to cater for, and not long after we were summoned to the house to have a large steak and a pile of chips. When dinner was over it was back to the winery, and we were all given jobs to do on the bottling line. It was a full-on job for the next four hours or so. One person handled empty bottles, one was on the filling machine — a very efficient siphoning unit — one on the corking machine, and one taking the full bottles away, with George supervising the jobs and making sure everything went smoothly. At other times of the year we would be asked if we would like to come and work in the vineyard, not only at Villa Maria but at other contract vineyards over at Kumeu, Whenuapai and even down south at Te Kauwhata. These were very enjoyable days and usually ended with a great barbecue and drinks.'

IN 1969, AS the new winery was coming on-stream and production was increasing, George offered Servantie a full-time role with the company as sales manager. After discussing it with his wife, Servantie accepted and started work at Villa Maria at the end of October that year. Servantie took his responsibilities very seriously and immediately immersed himself in the business. He quickly came to know the wines better than almost anyone apart from George himself.

'I worked in and around the winery, and also did local deliveries. In those days we had a short-wheel-base Ford F100 V8 flat-bed truck with a powerful engine and a very fierce clutch. It would hold four pallets of wine on the tray, but if they weren't roped on properly, or if you let the clutch out too quickly, you would spill two of the pallets off the back.'

At that time, shops in Auckland, the top half of the North Island and John Bull Wines in Wellington sold Villa Maria wines. It was Servantie's job to service these stores, as well as to expand the customer base throughout the rest of the country. Having no previous sales experience was no impediment; his highly organised approach provided Villa Maria with a new level of professionalism. The keys were organisation and thinking strategically; something that is often

Maurie Servantie, at right
in paisley shirt, leads one
of the regular wine-tasting
events at the winery.

harder than one imagines. Servantie made it look easy. His was a textbook lesson in the virtue of wearing out shoe leather when you are building a new business and introducing a totally unknown brand to the trade and consumers.

'I got hold of a wine booklet that listed all the liquor outlets in New Zealand, and with this I was able to make up lists of the different types of outlets — wine shops, wholesalers, pubs, restaurants, clubs and licensing trusts — in different areas of New Zealand,' he recalls. 'I mapped out an itinerary, and at the beginning of 1970 began my calling schedule. On all my circuits I used to send a card advising I would be in their particular area on a specific day. I sent out one-page notices to all the businesses I wanted to visit in any area, and told them when I would be in town. I organised to have price lists printed. Once we had established each one as a customer, this enabled them to prepare an order and organise any credits, etc. I also had cases of wine sent to storage depots in the area I was visiting to use as samples. George initially wasn't too keen on this approach, but I'm sure that being generous and handing out a mixed case of free wine to each of the outlets contributed hugely to the company getting its foot in the door of a good many outlets.'

Servantie's first trip was to Palmerston North on a Monday, where he picked up a rental car at the airport before travelling to the Wairarapa, Wellington and the Manawatu, then back to Palmerston North to catch a flight back to Auckland. 'It was a very unproductive week, but on reflection it was like so many first trips into the rest of the country. We were really just sowing seeds which we hoped would thrive and multiply.'

Each alternate week was spent in the Auckland area, while the rest of his time was spent travelling the length and breadth of the country. 'We spent a lot on rental-car mileage and Air New Zealand airfares over the next four years, but slowly and surely the word was spread.'

Wellington was always a good call for Maurie so far as George was concerned; it was one of the few places where Gorgonzola cheese could be bought in those days. The Dixon Street Deli always had a supply, and it was an understanding that Maurie brought some back for George in Auckland. Wellington was also always a good source of empty barrels, whether whisky, brandy, sherry or vermouth. They would be freighted back to Auckland, where George would have them steamed out by the winemaker, and the very tasty residue given to the staff.

ONE SIGNIFICANT ADVANTAGE for Maurie Servantie's sales efforts in the Wellington area was the support he had from Mike Aspros at John Bull Wines. Aspros had stocked Villa Maria wines for quite some time and knew George personally. He took Servantie around the various outlets in Wellington, introduced him, and let the owners know that he considered Villa Maria very good wine and well-priced. Their relationship has remained very close over the years, but there was one day when it was tested.

'The return leg of the South Island trip, the flight from Invercargill to Wellington, usually arrived about 6.30pm,' remembers Maurie. 'There was then an hour-and-a-half wait for the flight from Wellington to Auckland. On one trip Mike said he'd come out to the airport, pick me up and go for dinner somewhere to fill in the wait. I was quite surprised when after he picked me up we headed into Wellington city. I pointed out that I only had an hour-and-a-half, but he said that was plenty of time. He parked his car in an off-street car park in Bond Street and we walked around the corner to a Greek restaurant in the next street. We had a very hurried but enjoyable meal and walked back to the car. However, when we tried to get out of the car park the traffic wasn't moving, due to an accident in Willis Street. When we finally got moving, Mike drove like a Le Mans driver. How we ever got to the airport without an accident I'll never know! As my suitcase had been booked right through, all I had with me was my briefcase. I raced through the airport and along the boarding ramp, and shot through the first doorway and up the flight of stairs into the aircraft. You can imagine my surprise when I got to the top of the steps to find the aircraft was in total darkness. It was the wrong plane! So back down the steps and along the boarding ramp to the next gate — I just made it before they closed the doors. My heart was still going flat-out when we reached Auckland!'

ONCE HE HAD the North Island schedule sorted, Servantie began targeting the South Island. The size of his calling area meant that each trip took around two weeks instead of the usual one week, and even with the extra time the required schedule was tight enough to tax the most hardy salesperson.

'On Monday I would fly Auckland to Wellington, then catch a flight to Blenheim. I would pick up a rental car at the airport and do the Blenheim and Picton calls, then drive through to Havelock and on to Nelson, and do all the calls in the Nelson, Stoke and Richmond area. On the Wednesday, I would catch the Nelson Aero Club flight delivering newspapers to Westport, pick up another rental car at the airport, then do the calls in Westport and drive south to Greymouth. Then I would drive south to Hokitika and catch an Air New Zealand flight that same afternoon to Christchurch. That gave me Thursday, Friday, and Saturday in Christchurch and districts.

'On the following Monday I headed south to the Ashburton Licensing Trust and then into Timaru and Waimate, and finally the Oamaru Licensing Trust, arriving in Dunedin late in the day. Completing the rounds in Dunedin, I would drop the car and catch the Mount Cook flight to Queenstown, pick up another car, do the Queenstown calls and then drive to Alexandra, Gore and into Invercargill, before catching the Friday afternoon flight to Christchurch, on to Wellington, and back to Auckland and the winery for a big discussion with George.

'Again, on all my circuits I used to send a card advising that I would be in their particular area on a specific day. This enabled the customer to prepare an order and organise any credits, etc. The only wine licence on my call in Greymouth was at a Four Square supermarket. The husband and wife who ran it always knew I was pushed for time, as driving down from Westport and then on to Hokitika to catch the only afternoon flight to Christchurch didn't leave me a great deal of time at each call. So they always had an order written out, any credits listed, and — best of all — a big plate of whitebait sandwiches and a cup of coffee ready and waiting.'

Invercargill had its rewarding moments as well. 'In the early days, Invercargill was hard-going, as the wine licences in the city area were all under the Invercargill Licensing Trust domain, and orders had to be obtained at head office level and so were not very forthcoming. The saving grace was the one wine shop in the city where I got to know the lady owner quite well. Her husband was an oyster fisherman, and after our business relationship had developed I would often get a great feed of Bluff oysters.'

Troublesome customers were rare, and Maurie recalls a number of outstanding accounts, among them a wine shop in Waimate, owned and run by Eric and Thurza Batchelor. 'They really got behind our wines, and it got to the stage where I stayed at their home on the middle weekend when I did the South Island trip. The bonus was the fresh salmon that Eric Batchelor gave me that he caught in the Waitaki River.'

The Batchelors would often be invited to Villa Maria functions in Auckland as thanks for their support over the years. It wasn't until the death of Charles Upham VC and Bar that Servantie found out that Eric was now New Zealand's most decorated living soldier. He had the rare distinction of having received two awards of the Distinguished Conduct Medal (DCM), at that time the second-highest honour for bravery awarded to servicemen below the rank of commissioned officer in the British and Commonwealth armies.

SOMETIMES, THOUGH, the persuasive Servantie met his match. One customer was a Four Square supermarket on the outskirts of Invercargill, which had a wine licence and was independent of the all-powerful Licensing Trust. 'I was very lucky that on my first call I met up with the father of the three people who ran the outlet and obtained quite a decent order. However, when I called back on my next trip three weeks later I met up with his daughter,

Guests at the cellar door
in 1970. Some taste wine
while the gentleman at
left fills up his half-gallon
bottle with cream sherry.

who for some unknown reason had taken a dislike to Villa Maria, and told me that so far as she was concerned they wouldn't be buying any more Villa Maria products. The situation carried on for quite some time, and only changed when the daughter left to get married and moved away.'

Then there was the 'burning window display' episode. In the early 1970s one of Villa Maria's very successful lines was a product called Chassemino. 'The drawcard of this product was not only the blend of Chasselas and Palomino, but also its unique packaging,' Maurie recalls. 'This was a 1.5 litre carafe which not only looked very elegant, but also looked very similar to the famous squat Mateus Rosé carafe. (It was sealed with a screwcap, something that would figure prominently in Villa Maria's decision-making in the future).

'However, the carafe had an unforeseen flaw. I arranged a window display of Chassemino in a trust wine shop in the South Island, and went on my way, very happy with what I had accomplished. When I called in at the shop on my next trip, I thought the lady shopkeeper was going to tear my throat out. She yelled and raged, and when I finally got her to settle down I found out that my display of Chassemino carafes had nearly burnt the shop down! The window faced to the west, and the display carafes, which all had wine in them, had acted as magnifying glasses and burnt a series of arcs on the panelling at the back of the window and scorched a trail across the display posters. That was a near one!'

Maurie Servantie with
a wine-tasting customer
at the Villa Maria cellar
door, shortly after the
new winery opened.

7

TAKING IT
TO THE
NEXT LEVEL

George's remorseless drive for sales flowed over into family life. In 1968 the family had moved out of Kirkbride Road to Epsom for the sake of the children's schooling. Gail remained fully informed about what was happening and continued to play an active role, going out to the winery as often as she could, but she never returned to full-time work there. However, even in Epsom, 'there was no escaping it'.

A newly hirsute George
outside the winery. His
trusty blue Mercedes is
parked outside.

D uring the 11 years we spent in our first house, George's reps would always come and stay with us,' Gail remembers. 'The winemakers would be there, too; to reduce costs and help have extra training and conferences, George would insist that they stay with us when they came to Auckland for meetings and the like. I would put them all up. There were even a couple of Christmases when we hired a bach in Waipu for a holiday and we just about had the whole staff up there with us for New Year's Eve. They would come and pitch tents on our lawn.'

As the demand for Villa Maria wines grew, it became necessary to appoint distributors, particularly in the South Island. The first of these were Fletcher Humphries in Christchurch and Wilson Neill in Dunedin, Invercargill and Timaru. The support of these firms provided significant growth in sales for Villa Maria, and by the mid-1970s the sales team had grown and the company had representatives in Auckland, Waikato, Wellington and Christchurch. With the larger winery commissioned, and with the assistance of full-time winemaking and sales staff, George was able to turn his attention to expansion.

There was great energy and excitement throughout the industry. The poor-quality North American and European hybrid grape varieties were slowly being replaced by better classics such as Müller Thurgau, Gewürztraminer, Riesling and Cabernet Sauvingnon, and

One of the many wine-
industry tasting events
held at the winery
warehouse to promote
the Villa Maria brand.

A family dinner with
Mandica, at right, not long
before she died. From left
are Megan, Gail, Karen,
Michael and George.

grapes were seen as the new revenue-earner for farmers with surplus land. Intensive lobbying from the industry meant that licensing laws continued to be reviewed and loosened.

The consumer was kept up to date, too. The daily newspapers carried lengthy pieces on wine by the likes of Peter Saunders, who wrote in various suburban newspapers and magazines, Jock Graham of the *New Zealand Herald*, and Michael Brett of the *Auckland Star*; in fact, it could be argued that wine and wine matters received more coverage in the media then than they do now, even though the industry was so very much smaller. Wine was fast out-growing its 'novelty drink' phase.

And big business was starting to join the party. In 1969, Cooks New Zealand Wine Company had been established by a group of entrepreneurial Auckland businessmen, including John Fernyhough, and led by David Lucas. It became quickly renowned for high sales volume, driven by creative advertising campaigns never seen before in the New Zealand wine industry.

Cooks was the country's first publicly owned wine company, and in those days that made it very powerful. For the first time a serious amount of money was being poured into wine companies, and with this came competition — and inevitably tension — as the new kids on the block challenged the hegemony of the established.

Most of the action had been in Gisborne, where Montana was emerging rapidly. Frank Yukich had purchased local producer Waihirere Wines to establish a base in Gisborne, and not long after built a new Montana winery there. One of Montana's first strategies when it moved into the province was to increase the price paid to winegrowers in order to attract more growers and increase supply. 'It was usual to have caps on tonnages, but Frank changed this,' says George. 'There was a battle between Corbans and Montana over this. Corbans was cropping four tons to the acre, so Montana went open slather and took over suppliers. Industry sources believed it was in response that the Corbans family brought in outside shareholders, and then in 1970 sold 70 per cent of the company to Rothmans.' (Rothmans purchased the remaining 30 per cent of Corbans in 1979.)

From the start, Villa Maria was a keen sponsor — here of the Miss Waihi Beach contest — of events that would appeal to new young wine consumers.

Michael Cooper's *The Wines and Vineyards of New Zealand* notes that vineyard acreage tripled between 1965 and 1970 as contract-growing swept the Gisborne plains. An average winery bought in 4 per cent of its grape requirements in 1960. By 1990, 460 independent growers produced 77 per cent of all New Zealand grapes, including 88 per cent of bulk wine grapes and 63 per cent of premium-wine varieties. Wine production would increase between 1960 and 1983 from 4.1 million litres to 57.7 million litres per annum.

New regions were also coming on-stream. As already noted, Marlborough had been identified as a very promising area for growing grapes based on the work Wayne Thomas had done for Frank Yukich, and in 1973 Montana — now 40 per cent owned by international drinks company Seagram — purchased large tracts of Marlborough for planting in grapes. That same year Peter Hubscher became Montana's operations manager, and under the influence of Seagram introduced new winemaking techniques. The confidence that Corban's Alex Corban and Montana's Frank and Mate Yukich had shown in the late 1960s in the Gisborne region's capacity to grow good quality Müller Thurgau grapes was beginning to prove accurate. In addition, new benchmark table wines, such as Gisborne Chardonnay, were completely changing the way consumers perceived wine.

Activity was building up in Hawke's Bay as well, as winemakers discovered the area's rich but almost forgotten winemaking heritage. The first of this new generation, John Buck and Michael Morris, had purchased the long-established Chambers vineyard near Havelock North and created Te Mata Estate in 1974. It was the birth and rebirth of Hawke's Bay wineries that would forge a reputation for tremendous wines, including Chardonnay, Cabernet Sauvignon and Merlot. George would soon join it.

UP UNTIL THIS TIME the industry had been noted for its collegiality, but business was business, and before long the gloves would come off. 'McWilliam's thought I was putting up prices for the Müller Thurgau [grapes] I was getting out of Hawke's Bay by 15 to 20 per cent,' George remembers. 'McWilliam's [the creation of a 1962 amalgamation of Australian producer McWilliam's Wines and the iconic Hawke's Bay winery McDonald's], put their prices up to try and compete with the prices they thought I was paying. But it was only a rumour. I was paying $300 per ton for Müller Thurgau, which was the going rate. What I was doing was paying growers to plant more varieties. The very astute Tom McDonald [a pioneer in the New Zealand wine industry, who at 19 years of age had established his own winery in 1927 by purchasing the Hawke's Bay business of his employer, Bartholomew Steinmetz] was still a big factor in the district at the time. Most of the growers supplying other companies would say there was no money in planting different varieties "because Tom said so". When McDonald was CEO of McWilliam's he was, I suppose understandably, fiercely competitive and gave little support to newcomers from Auckland. However, when he became chairman of New Zealand Winegrowers he was superb, taking an entirely independent approach and working very hard for the good of the entire industry.'

By the mid-1970s the 'bag-in-the-box' cask delivery of wine pioneered by Montana was also in full flight. It was convenient in more ways than one: as New Zealand wine production grew, winemakers were faced with increasing supplies of wine and had to find ways of shifting more volume. 'The Australians had already worked out that cardboard casks were an effective way of delivering cheaper wine to the consumer, and they were reputed to be selling more than 60 per cent of their production in three- and four-litre casks,' says George. 'Although it went against my better judgement, when the big New Zealand companies took up the idea Villa Maria was eventually forced to put in a separate packaging line and produce wine in this way. Nobilo's, Pacific Vineyards and Delegat's followed suit, and eventually casks accounted for more than 50 per cent of local sales. But I was determined that we would put the best wine possible in the cask, and we took particular care to ensure that retailers knew that stock rotation was important to ensure that the quality and integrity of our wines stayed intact.'

It's hard to imagine now, but by the late 1970s the fridges of most middle-class homes had a box of 'cask white' on their shelves, and almost every kitchen had a bottle of cask red on the bench. In typical fashion, to compete George had gone all-out on cask wine, and eventually Villa Maria was offering in excess of 15 different separate cask wines and categories under three brands. They included the widely popular Maison Vin, a four-litre blend of Chasselas and Müller Thurgau. Another was labelled Brookvale, a Riesling Sylvaner (the new name the industry had started to give Müller Thurgau) that was also packaged in a more compact three-litre cask. Villa Value offered Camberley Dry White, made from Chasselas, Chardonnay and Chenin Blanc. To top it all off there was even an especially-made 1.5-litre Villa Maria glass decanter available.

But cask-wine sales began to have a hugely negative effect on the sales of Villa Maria's bottled varietals which, eventually had to come down in price to offer any competition at all. In this George was not alone; looming on the horizon for an industry that was otherwise surging ahead was a price crisis.

BY THE MID-1970S Villa Maria was sitting at number five in terms of volume of wine produced, close in size to Hawke's Bay-based Glenvale, which at the time was also a relatively large producer. But these two were still well behind the big four of Montana, McWilliam's, Corbans and Penfolds New Zealand. They were big companies, with considerable muscle. To compete, a winery had to get into the wholesale market, but Villa Maria found it tough going; it was all very tightly held. Dominion Breweries and Lion Breweries were firmly ensconced in the wine trade through their respective shareholdings in Montana (Lion via Campbell and Ehrenfried) and McWilliam's and Penfolds (Dominion Breweries), and permitted their hotels and wholesalers to stock only wines from the local companies in which they had an interest or wines that they imported. Villa Maria was struggling to get a foothold.

And George couldn't have worked any harder. The company owned 15 acres at Kirkbride Road, and had around 150 acres in Hawke's Bay and 150 acres in Gisborne under contract. Production stood at 150,000 cases a year. George was a one-man whirlwind: doing the viticulture, liaising with growers and organising delivery of grapes, and supervising the winemaking team. (For the 1974 vintage, after Ross Spence left, George had even taken over as winemaker again for a time, working with Jimmy Green.) The multiplicity of his roles was all-consuming, and George was frustrated by Villa Maria's comparative lack of size. He was doing around 1350 tons a year; Montana was doing 5000 tons. But he had ways of punching above his weight.

'Despite the big guys, we were really making a difference in the market, especially because of our approach to marketing, training and sales. With an effective sales force to service them, we formed a lot of strong associations with independent, family-owned wine shops. I had an ability to get things done. It was easy for me to organise people and get them to do the things that needed to be done even though I was doing stuff on instinct more than anything,' he says.

In 1977 Villa Maria shared a stand with the New Zealand Dairy Board at the Wellington Trade Fair. Together they made quite an impact, Villa Maria handing out wine samples and the Dairy Board handing out cheese. The exposure Villa Maria got at the show created a tremendous demand for its wine, and within a week of the show finishing the sales team started to get orders from both DB and Lion outlets. Not long after, George was approached by wholesalers who wanted to take control of Villa Maria's distribution. 'My attitude was, they wouldn't help me when I was small, so why, when I'd worked hard to develop an alternate route to market, should I accommodate them now?' he remembers.

As the independent wine sellers had become stronger, they began to be less influenced by the larger brewery-controlled wholesalers for supply and more open to buying direct from producers. George and Maurie Servantie were seen as being the most proactive in convincing retailers to buy direct from the winery, by-passing wholesalers, and in some shops this helped Villa Maria reach a level of 30 per cent of the local wine sold. This made George very unpopular with both wholesalers and breweries, who saw this encroachment and competition into what they considered their territory as predatory.

The success of the sales and promotion regime instituted by Maurie Servantie continued to be effective, and by the late 1970s the company had reps throughout the country. Their regular call cycles, plus many in-store tastings, greatly improved Villa Maria's ability to service the customers and, with a positive response to a new label from customers, the reputation of the brand continued to flourish.

The South Island was covered by Lynn Wirth, who was based in Christchurch; the lower North Island was covered by Kevin Aitkin; Cherie Beard, based in Hamilton, covered the Waikato, Bay of Plenty and Taranaki; and Auckland and Northland were looked after by Bruce Quedley and Anne Iremonger, Gail Fistonish's sister. 'There was no formal hierarchy,' remembers Servantie, 'but as the longest-serving rep and sales manager I was always around to give advice and assistance where required. When I was not available, everyone reported directly to George.'

There were sales successes beyond the confines of the wine stores and wholesalers. A chance conversation with a member of the New Zealand Navy resulted in Villa Maria supplying the naval base at Devonport with wines for the Navy's ships, and not long after that the company managed to supply some cruise ships which were making regular appearances in Auckland.

But not all Villa Maria's customers were reliable. In Auckland, one plush restaurant, Bonaparte's, had run up a substantial account and was very reluctant to pay. George took a number of his sales team, plus their wives, to dinner one night and the party ate and drank up large. On leaving, George said, 'Take the bill off the account you owe Villa Maria.'

Servantie remembers only one other bad account, a small wine shop in Foxton. 'The owner's name was Sims but he changed it to Goldie, after the famous painter. He did paintings that were forgeries of famous Goldies, which he displayed in his shop. He gave me an order for about 40 cartons on my first call in 1970, and everyone thought this was going to be a first-class outlet. Then it was brought to my attention that he hadn't paid his account, so when I was in the

In the thick of it: George
with assistant winemaker
Jimmy Green.

area I pointed this out to him. He was very apologetic and gave me a cheque for the amount there and then. The staff cheered when I got back to Villa — but the cheers died when the cheque bounced! It took a long time for him to square our account.

'Another unusual customer was a restaurant in Turangi. The first orders were very ordinary, and then after a couple of months we got a large order for one of our very standard red wines, called "Dry Red". A lot later we found out that the restaurant was on-selling it to the cooks at the Italian camp at nearby Tokaanu where the men working on the hydro scheme were billeted.'

Competition among wine companies was strong, but it was also a time when travelling wine representatives got along very well — until the tougher atmosphere of the industry that had developed by the late 1970s intervened. 'In the early 1970s the reps of the different wine companies would often go out of our way to help each other out,' remembers Maurie Servantie. 'It was quite a usual practice for reps to get together for a drink and a yack at the offices of one of the companies on a Friday afternoon. Sadly, by the middle of the 1970s this practice was frowned upon by the bigger companies and it came to a screaming halt.'

After-work drinks at the
Seppelts Vidal cellar door
in the late 1970s. Note
the walk socks and shorts.

8
CRITICAL
MASS

In 1974, with Ross Spence gone, George did the vintage himself with the assistance of the cellar hands. 'It was like going back to the past. I had stayed involved in actually making wine, but had been less hands-on. While I enjoyed immensely being back on the tools, it was clear I couldn't do both jobs. I immediately set about trying to find another winemaker.'

This wine has been made from late picked Cabernet Sauvignon grapes selected from the Vidal vineyards of Te Moana, Te Mata & Havelock in the celebrated Hawkes Bay district of New Zealand. Late picking and favourable vintage conditions have made this wine ready for consumption at a comparatively young age. It is an extremely delicate wine showing signs of complexity with a clean firm finish. It has a taste and flavour characteristic of Cabernet Sauvignon grown in Hawkes Bay. This wine will improve with further bottle age. Store lying down.

VIDAL
Private Bin 1977
Cabernet Sauvignon

CONTENTS 750 ml PRODUCED BY SEPPELT VIDAL HASTINGS LTD
ALC. CONT. 11·5% BY VOL. APPROX.

A nd as he laboured in the winery over the Pinotage from Captain Mick Walker's vineyard at Whenuapai (a varietal at that point produced predominantly by Nobilo's), the Cabernet, some Chardonnay and the Müller Thurgau, it was also clear to George that he couldn't sit still and continue to be out-muscled by the big guys. Just as he had expanded back in 1969 when he had bought more land at Mangere, now he needed more capacity, and a more secure supply of grapes than could be guaranteed with winegrower contracts alone. His constant search for grapes had involved a good deal of travel throughout the North Island in his trusty blue Mercedes Benz; trips to the Hawke's Bay would take him around six hours.

George needed to grow to achieve the critical mass so important to his survival, and eventually in Hawke's Bay he identified the Hastings-based Seppelt Vidal, established by Anthony Vidal in 1905, as an opportunity for that expansion.

Vidal had a remarkable history, dating back to Spaniard immigrant Jose Sole, who anglicised his name to Joseph Soler when he planted vines near Wanganui. In 1906, as recounted by Dick Scott in the seminal book *Winemakers of New Zealand*, there was a sensation at the Christchurch International Exhibition when Soler's wines won three gold medals from the five offered, in competition with overseas exhibitors. Leading Australian winemakers protested at this result, and a special meeting of Cabinet ordered a re-judging by an expert approved by the Australians. This time, Soler's wines took all five gold medals. In 1888 Soler brought his nephew, Anthony Vidal, to New Zealand to help him in his wine business. It was the nephew who in the early 1900s moved to Hastings, planting vines and establishing the winery which bears his name.

George knew the company and its business well, as he was already buying Hawke's Bay Müller Thurgau grapes from Vidal. He knew that as a grape supplier Vidal was marginally profitable, and that it had benefited from management systems implemented by Seppelt of Australia, who had bought a 60 per cent share from the Vidal family in 1972, only to sell it a couple of years later to the manager, Ross McLennan. McLennan had contracts with a great number of growers and had plenty of grapes for himself and for Villa Maria.

This arrangement provided Villa Maria with important extra volume, but it became apparent early on that it wasn't going to be enough, that the company would need a physical base in Hawke's Bay. In 1976 George bought Seppelt Vidal from McLennan for $30,000 — not the land or buildings, just the business and stock. This immediately provided Villa Maria with 100 acres of Riesling and Müller Thurgau grapes as well as a small quantity of Merlot and Cabernet. It was just the explosion of new varieties that George wanted, but first he had to fight with his bank to finance the deal. The National Bank did not see the logic in buying Vidal, so he went to the BNZ. It was a tough decision. The National Bank had been his parents' bank for years, and the Villa Maria bank from the day he set the company up in 1961. However, grapes are the lifeblood of a wine company, and if he was to succeed he had no choice. He has had, by his own admission, 'quite a history of changing banks when they don't agree with logical business strategies' since.

A YEAR LATER he bought the rest — the land and buildings — and reverted to the solely Vidal brand. He knew he would have to take Vidal in a new direction. First under Seppelt and then later under McLennan, when its standard lines were dropped and labels changed, the appeal

George with Prime
Minister Rob Muldoon
and his wife Thea at the
opening of the Vidal's
winery restaurant, a first
for New Zealand.

of the brand had declined. Without intervention profitability would remain poor, but George had no intention of closing it down. 'It was such a beautiful old winery with its barrel hall. The first thing after I bought it was to have a massive clean-out. The winery had been let go a bit and was very untidy. There was rubbish and junk everywhere. But it was also fairly highly automated so far as wineries in Hawke's Bay went. They had a portable crushing plant and limited refrigeration, so we put in a new crushing plant and more cool storage.'

When George purchased Vidal, the winemaker was Warwick Orchiston, who had joined the company in 1971. George saw no need at the time to change the winemaker. 'He was doing a pretty good job, and I was down there a lot so I kept on eye on things.'

And George had great plans for Vidal. In 1979, after overcoming objections from neighbours and a two-year battle with the various local and licensing authorities, a licence was granted to operate a vineyard bar restaurant in the Vidal barrel room in Hastings. It was a first for the country.

It is hard to imagine now, but the whole enterprise was clearly regarded with a great deal of suspicion. Reading the coverage in the local paper — carefully clipped by George's PA Gail Harding and pasted into one of the many press-clippings scrapbooks George has kept — it becomes clear that many local residents and bureaucrats couldn't even *imagine* that there could be any attraction in having a glass of wine with a meal in pleasant surroundings. The licence was issued with tough restrictions: the restaurant had to stop serving by 9pm and everyone had to be off the premises by 9.30pm. But even these minor irritants could not disguise the fact that in opening the restaurant in Vidal's lovely old barrel hall George had once again shown great vision.

New Zealand's first licensed vineyard bar and restaurant was officially opened in grand style, with plenty of local dignitaries and media invited, and Prime Minister the Right Honourable Robert Muldoon officiating.

Gail Fistonich remembers the event and how it was yet another case of how, when George was intensely focused, the business came first and other details became a little vague. George had suggested that because it was school holidays Gail bring the children and her mother down for the opening. 'George told me he was flying down early to get things ready and said I could have a nice relaxing drive down in the Mercedes,' Gail recalls. 'We set out about two or three in the afternoon with no idea of how far we had to go. The Mercedes was a real gas-guzzler, and by the time I got to the middle of the Taupo–Napier Road I was practically empty of petrol. Anyway, we got to Napier, and I always remember seeing the airport and thinking, "I will kill George for not getting us here the easy way."

In Napier we pulled up by a taxi and I asked the driver where Vidal's was and he said, "Oh, lady, that's in Hastings." I had no clue how far Hastings was, and was annoyed that we had travelled all that way and still had further to go. George had casually said to just come down for the night! Well, there was no way that was going to happen, so we stayed for a few days. George was a terror for doing things like that. He could jump on a plane, but would not stop to think of how much hassle it was for us to do things.'

It was an occasion remembered, too, by Bob and Marion Campbell, who were instrumental in assisting with establishing the restaurant. At the time Bob Campbell, now a well-known wine writer and judge, was working for Villa Maria, looking after the company's four House of Wine retail shops and some public relations activity. A few weeks after he started work, and in anticipation of the formal opening, George had added the responsibility for opening the Vidal restaurant to Campbell's list of tasks. Campbell, who was based in Auckland, travelled to Hastings only to find what he describes as an 'utter shambles . . . Nothing had been done. The staff hadn't ordered furniture; the kitchen was not set up properly; and really it was in no fit state to open.'

One of the first things Bob Campbell did was recruit a new restaurant team by putting out an advertisement over the local radio station. 'I called Marion and flew her down from Auckland to give me a hand. She took over the back of house, organising food platters, while I worked on sorting out front of house. George arranged for his friend Tony White's (of the famous Tony's Restaurants) brother

Paul, who was a chef, to come down, and between the three of us we managed to cobble together a very respectable restaurant. The opening day was chaotic, but nobody apart from us knew that. We had both television channels present, which was quite a coup, and the Prime Minister to open it.'

'For a number of years after we opened it,' says George, 'the very successful restaurant at Vidal's was visited by many other wine companies looking to establish a vineyard restaurant, but it stayed the only one for about the next five years. It set a high standard, and since then vineyard restaurants and cafés have become a huge asset to the industry.'

His time in Hastings gave Campbell the view that the region needed an organisation of some kind to represent local winemakers, so he called a number of them to a meeting at Vidal's. 'I told them to bring a bottle and we would discuss my idea of an association. What resulted was Hawke's Bay Vintners, with John Buck of Te Mata as the first president and me as the first secretary.'

Campbell also recalls that Warwick Orchiston had some 'zany ideas about making wine. I know he was having trouble getting the budget to buy some more barrels. At some point he came across an oak tree and took off a branch and soaked it in wine, a precursor I guess to using the oak staves. I'm not sure if he was serious or was just making a point.'

Campbell left Villa Maria to take up 'a once in a lifetime opportunity with Corbans in Los Angeles'. He was, in 2005, to become the first-ever recipient of the George Fistonich Medal, which is awarded annually at the New Zealand International Wine Awards, organised by Kingsley Woods, and which recognises outstanding contributions to the New Zealand wine industry.

NOT ALL GROWERS under contract to Vidal had wanted initially to continue the arrangement with Villa Maria, but George was his usual persuasive self and eventually the majority signed on. One dispute did go to arbitration before agreement was reached, however. Many of the growers had surplus land, and so there was further opportunity for George to increase plantings and increase his supply of Müller Thurgau and Chasselas grapes, and to also try to persuade the growers to try new varietals.

'Müller Thurgau and Chasselas were easy to grow, easy-care and high cropping, and made growers good money,' he explains. 'This may explain why some were reluctant to go with the alternative varietals, such as Riesling, Chardonnay, Cabernet Sauvingnon and Merlot, that we wanted, but preferred to stay with what they knew.' Even so, George persuaded many growers that these alternative varieties would pay off. Later, Villa Maria planted Chardonnay and more Bordeaux-type reds, and in the end George had increased his supply by about 50 per cent.

In 1977 Villa Maria used Vidal grapes for the first time, when George and Warwick Orchiston made Vidal Steiner, a sparkling Müller Thurgau. They also made Mount Erin Müller Thurgau and Tomoana Riesling, as well as small quantities of Cabernet and Chardonnay. The fruit was crushed in Hawke's Bay, and the wine made there, but George had decided to close down the Vidal bottling plant and bring the juice to Auckland for bottling. Vidal was still making sherry and port, and some of the grapes were used for that, too.

The combined operations were startlingly versatile. Villa Maria was also making two ports, six sherries, four sparkling wines, and wines labelled 'Moselwein', 'Hock', 'Sauternes', 'Burgundy', 'Claret' and 'Seibel Red'. What was generally not known was that George was also experimenting. He was making tiny batches of Pinotage, Melesconera, Riesling, Cabernet Sauvignon, Chardonnay and Pinot Noir from grapes grown in the Henderson, Kumeu and Te Kauwhata areas. Not all of these varietals would make it onto shop shelves, but it was a strong signal that George's penchant for finding wines to satisfy growing consumer interest while at the same time creating a strong point of distinction between himself and his competitors was stronger than ever.

George did a great deal of the viticulture himself — as he describes it, 'screaming around the growers', particularly in the Gisborne and Hawke's Bay regions. Then, as the 1980s rolled around, he employed Debbie Reid as his first viticulturist. Reid, who had a BSc Hons degree and was passionate about wine and highly focused on quality, had a great influence on improved grape quality in the vineyards and the supply from growers. 'Debbie came on board at just the right time, and I cannot over-estimate the contribution she made,' George says.

It was during Reid's period with the company that George achieved yet another first by initiating New Zealand's first grower bonus system, which rewarded growers for the quality of their grapes, not simply for the quantity produced.

Reid (now Gilchrist) had come back to Auckland after working in various wineries over several vintages in Europe and California. A cellar position was available at Villa Maria and she found herself involved in the 1981 vintage. 'In Germany and California I had worked in very modern wineries,' she remembers. 'Back then the Villa Maria plant was old and piecemeal. The laboratory hung above the boiler, which would often vent its steam, causing us to sway. After some negotiation with management we cordoned off an area as an office so we could hear one another speak. In today's world the old winery would never have passed a health and safety check. However, it was a great experience as we had to cover all jobs, whether that meant pulling a pump apart or giving a wine tasting.'

Reid's first vintage with Villa Maria highlighted the need to raise the quality of the grapes, so she returned to Geisenheim, Germany, for a year's study, arranged through Dr Helmut Becker, who was a great fan of New Zealand and a fantastic mentor and host to Reid and other New Zealanders. 'As I was supporting myself I worked at the Hangs Lang Weingut in Hattenheim and for a whole year tended a four-hectare vineyard as well as working in the winery,' she says. 'This allowed me to gain first-hand experience of looking after a vineyard while attending lectures and debating trellising styles, spraying regimes and so on, as well as gaining increased knowledge of winemaking techniques. I travelled to France with Dr Becker and other winemaking students, where the main focus was on vineyards and grape varieties. I still recall the day that Dr Becker strode into a vineyard in Beaujolais, grabbed a bunch of grapes and crushed them. Bright red juice streamed from his fingers and he said words to the effect, "This is how the French get colour in their red wines."'

These experiences were invaluable when Reid returned to New Zealand 18 months later. 'It gave me the confidence to establish a viticultural position at Villa Maria, when the industry was still in its infancy,' she says. As well as also doing the lab tests and working in the cellar, on two occasions Reid filled in as manager for the Vidal's complex. 'Flexibility was the name of the game,' she says. 'After my experiences overseas, I realised I had been naive in thinking that New Zealand growers knew how to grow grapes for winemaking. Many New Zealand growers thought that the grapes should be green when harvested, and had little understanding of the relationship between sugar content, pH and acid levels. Some felt a 60 per cent loss of grafted root stock was acceptable.' Thus the process of grower education began.

Reid held wine tastings with the growers, introducing them to wines and explaining how different qualities were achieved. Regular information sheets were provided on recognising a good graft and how to plant them. Specific Villa rather than chemical-company spray schedules were introduced, as were such practices as leaf plucking, using flame-throwers instead of herbicides, planting green manure crops between the rows, and many other techniques that are now standard.

'As the company viticulturist I became well acquainted with growers and their vineyards,' she remembers. 'Grape growing was a relatively new experience for growers, and many had little understanding of the diseases and how they affected grape vines. The chemical companies had a field day with spray schedules that required use of their products every two weeks. My experiences overseas had highlighted the need to work towards a more "organic" approach, and with the rise of exports many sprays were automatically banned.'

Reid recalls a visit from a chemical company, 'two bright young lads, pushing their products. I mentioned the need to consider a more healthy approach. They left, and unaware that I was behind them, I caught them mumbling "Silly bitch". Good communication over many cups of coffee, and a few glasses of wine, helped growers to trust your decisions, and after four years the task was much easier.'

She remembers the 1980s as an exciting time to be in the industry. 'Familiar faces included Dr Richard Smart and Rainer Eschenbruch, with their research work at the Te Kauwhata Research Station; winemakers such as James Millton, who allowed me to observe the outcome of biodynamic practices; Joe Corban with his grafting operation; Denis Irwin and Hatsch Kalberer, who kindly let me use Matawhero winery to undertake all my grape testing in Gisborne; and of course all the dedicated Villa Maria and Vidal's growers. Everyone seemed keen to share their experiences, knowledge and expertise and there was a great fraternity with a desire to learn and make excellent wines.

'Once growers were willing to hold their grapes on for added ripeness, the additional costs of growing needed to be taken into account to cover additional vineyard work, spraying and shrinkage. Finding a fair price for wine grapes became important and was a constant source of aggravation between growers and wineries. In a free market, supply and demand works well, until there is a surplus or a shortage. However, if a winery wants particular grape varieties and needs a specific tonnage then they need to have growers who will provide what they want. When I left Villa Maria I felt we had come up with something equitable.'

In 1987 Reid informed George of her desire to change direction, and gave him notice of her intention to leave for a position at the Kiwifruit Marketing Board. George asked her to find a replacement; not an easy task given the shortage of qualified viticulturists in New Zealand. Eventually she identified Steve Smith, a young man working at the Department of Agriculture under Dr Richard Smart, who was a well-known and highly regarded viticulturist. Reid and George approached Smith only to find that he had been offered a job at the Cloudy Bay winery in Marlborough. George convinced Smith that he would gain more experience working at Villa Maria, where they were making a wider variety of wine than any other company, using grapes from Hawke's Bay, Te Kauwhata, Auckland and Gisborne, and were about to expand rapidly into the Marlborough region. In addition, George told Smith he would be working alongside Kym

Milne, already a highly awarded winemaker. Smith was eventually convinced by George's declaration that this offered him a better career path, and in 1988 he joined Villa, working for a short time as Reid's assistant before taking over as senior viticulturist.

Smith (who is now the director of winemaking and viticulture at Craggy Range) stayed with Villa Maria until 1998, and George regarded him as a real asset, who forged a reputation as a highly intelligent viticulturist and an enthusiastic promoter of New Zealand wine. 'He is very well connected, and is perhaps one of the most recognised New Zealand wine personality overseas,' says George.

DURING THE MID-1970S Villa Maria wines continued to win awards at wine shows around the country, including a string of gold medals for its Sauternes (then the term for a range of late-harvest or sweet wines), and in 1979 Villa Maria dominated the awards at the Trade and Industry Wine Show. George was driven to make the best, and to experiment with new varietals. He had managed to gain access to small quantities of Pinotage, Cabernet Sauvignon and Chardonnay grapes, and his Gisborne growers were supplying him with Müller Thurgau, then considered best suited for making top-end table wine. (During the 1970s, almost 50 per cent of the New Zealand wines sold in restaurants were made predominantly from Müller Thurgau, and sold as Liebestraum, Bernkastel and so on. This was the era of pretentious, *faux* European names being given to New Zealand wines, many of which, says George, bore only a faint resemblance to their classic, continental namesakes.)

With changes in licensing laws leading to the opening of more and more licensed restaurants, George knew that access to Müller Thurgau was vital to his being able to be a part of this growing market. After all, Nobilo's Müller Thurgau, produced by Nick Nobilo, was widely considered to be a market leader in its time. And George did not want to sit in the middle of the pack. By the mid- to late 1970s he had released premium varietals under both the Villa Maria and Vidal brands and, although these were still in very small quantities, their very existence was setting George apart from many other boutique wineries and leading him into more direct competition with the larger producers. Importantly, too, the purchase of Vidal not only expanded Villa Maria's wine portfolio, it also led to one of the most innovative and successful national marketing campaigns the New Zealand wine industry had ever experienced.

In 1977, George and his still-small staff decided to use an innovative event to bring Villa Maria and Vidal to the attention of every wine outlet in the country, by holding a series of Croation-style lamb-on-the-spit barbecues around the country. Although the wines were being made separately by different winemaking teams, the sales team was marketing the Villa Maria and Vidal brands together; they had heritage and history, so it seemed the rational thing to do. It was decided that Villa Maria would undertake an ambitious road trip, beginning in Dunedin and travelling on to Christchurch, Wellington, Hastings and Auckland. They wrote to every licence-holder in the country and invited them to a barbecue at the venue closest to them.

Maurie Servantie played a crucial part in the planning and execution of the event. What was to be a nine-day road-show 'was all planned with military precision. We worked out that it would take at least 12 people to execute the plan. We didn't have 12 sales staff at that time, so we asked for volunteers from other areas of the company. Needless to say we had no trouble getting volunteers. We planned to start the barbecues in July — not the warmest month — so they didn't clash with Villa Maria's vintage work and bottling programmes, or with the pre-Christmas activities of the guests. Four hundred turned up in Dunedin, another 600 in Christchurch, 600 in Wellington, 350 in Hawke's Bay and about 1300 in Auckland. It involved cooking about 150 lambs, and nothing like it had ever been done.

'It didn't all go smoothly: pallets of wine along with all the other gear needed to put on a genuine barbecue of roast lamb on the spits had been dispatched to Dunedin a couple of weeks before the event, just as the seamen on the inter-island ferries decided to go on strike. At the last minute a decision was made to air-freight everything down. The cost of this South Island barbecue shot through the ceiling, as

Lambs on the spit at one
of the famous Villa Maria
travelling barbecues.

you can imagine. The Dunedin event was to be held at Larnach Castle, and Carol Thomas [later Payne] and Paul White, from Tony's restaurant, flew down from Auckland several days beforehand to get everything organised and purchase the lambs, wood, vegetables and salads. The rest of the team arrived the night before to assist Paul with the preparation. The fires were all arranged ready to be lit at 6.30am, so that the lambs could be starting to cook before 8am. It turned out that the power-points were in a locked shed, and it wasn't possible to contact Larnach Castle staff until quite late, which threw the cooking programme off-schedule. This was compounded by the extra-heavy lambs that had been supplied for the Dunedin shindig. They took an extra two hours to cook, which hadn't been factored into the planning.

'Our customers had arrived around 11am and immediately got stuck into the wine, and by the time lunch was served everyone was in very high spirits, having a great time. The show proved to be a tremendous success. After it was all over, George thought it would be a good idea if I did a tour of the South Island to determine the response level. It was overwhelmingly positive, and resulted in a huge increase in sales. People were still talking about the Villa barbecues years later.'

Importantly, the tour broke the sales drought in areas of the South Island, where licensing trusts were dominant, and signalled the beginning of the trend towards trade support from larger retail liquor stores. The barbecues had a thawing effect on what had at times been tense relationships. To cement the thaw, the different trusts were invited to Auckland one at a time. The Villa Maria team would meet them at the airport, bring them to the winery for lunch, show them around, and then in the afternoon arrange for another winery to pick them up and take them elsewhere. They left Villa Maria with gifts of wine and a fond farewell, and sales to the trusts improved even further.

These events were not without their entertainments. George remembers one woman guest in particular. 'This woman, who owned a chain of wine shops, had a bone to pick with the marketing manager from a well-known Dunedin-based wholesaler who had been an early promoter of discounting. After a few drinks she decided this was an

Tony's restaurant, in
Auckland, was an early
and loyal supporter of
Villa Maria's wines.

appropriate time to make her point, that discounting was foreign to Dunedin. She spotted a guy with a large bushy beard whom she thought was the culprit and duly poured a large glass of wine over him. Unfortunately the man she chose, although similar in looks, was not her intended target but a young journalist from a local Dunedin radio station, and he was not amused.'

GAIL FISTONICH HAS her own recollection of 'special events' with George. The annual wine awards at the Chateau Tongariro was a popular event for winemakers and their partners, who were then a smaller and closer community. They would gather for the weekend to eat and drink and find out which of their wines had been successful.

One year George decided that he and Gail would drive to the Chateau in the Mercedes, taking with them Joyce Harris, the wife of wine writer Stanley Harris, who was also attending. 'Joyce was probably in her seventies and very flamboyant,' remembers Gail. 'On the way down we got a puncture. Joyce was sitting in the back all done up like a duchess. George got out and took the wheel off, and the car began to roll forward. Joyce just sat there looking very regal. Unfortunately George had forgotten that the spare also had a puncture, and when he got back into the car he looked absolutely sick.

'We limped into Taupo and got to the service station at around 5.30pm, as it was about to close. For some reason they asked George to open the bonnet, and when he said he couldn't because the latch was broken I thought, this is the last straw. They fixed the tyre and gave us a spare, which for some reason we had to put on the back seat next to Joyce, and I can always remember her sitting there like a duchess, with her hand on the tyre to keep it from touching her dress. When we got to the Chateau, Stanley was waiting on the steps, clearly worried about why the journey had taken so long. Joyce just looked at George and said, "I think we might keep this story to ourselves." It was absolutely beautiful, but that's George — great at the big picture, but never one for taking care of the little practical things around the house. And yet quality and detail was a real strength of his around the winery.'

The Villa Maria stand
at an A&P show.

9
SNOWDROPPERS
AND SYLVANER

In 1977 the amiable Harry Wright was the winemaker at Villa Maria, working alongside George. George's nephew Fabian Yukich (a son of George's sister Elsie and her ex-husband Frank Yukich), who would soon become cellar supervisor, started at Villa Maria on the same day.

Harry Wright at work
in the winery.

F abian Yukich worked in the winery, ran the distillery, and also did some of the lab work. He soaked up the winemaking knowledge. 'I credit Harry for teaching me the importance of cleanliness in the winery,' he says. 'Harry used to tell me, "If we keep everything spotlessly clean, we won't create problems that I don't have the education to solve." It was a lesson I never forgot, even later when I left Villa to return to work with my father.'

It was a small team: George, Harry, Fabian and a couple of cellar hands. Harry's skill came not from a set of formal winemaking qualifications, but from the years of experience he had picked up while working for the Brajkovich family's San Marino Vineyards (later to become Kumeu River) and for the Nobilo family at its wineries in West Auckland.

George was on a mission, and was looking to add further strength to the team. So in June he offered Mark Polglase, a young university graduate with a double degree in chemistry and microbiology, a job working in the cellar and helping out Englishman Mike Bennett, who had joined the company a few months earlier as an assistant winemaker.

Polglase had recently returned from a job-hunting holiday in Australia and was considering offers from both Villa Maria and Lion Breweries. 'I was actually inclined towards the one at Lion, but they wouldn't take me for three weeks, and as I had only $80 to my name

I needed something sooner so I could survive. When I told the guys at Lion why I had made the decision to take the job at Villa they said that if it didn't work out then I could go back and see them in 18 months' time and they would give me a job as a trainee brewer. Needless to say I never went back to them.'

During vintage, winemaking at Villa Maria was organised in two shifts: the first began at 7.30am, and the second at 3pm. In those days everyone, including George, lent their hands to whatever task was required. Polglase was immediately put onto the night shift, and spent his first few months with the company working alongside Bennett and, amongst other winemaking tasks, bottling sherry. (Although fortifieds were in decline, the wine industry as a whole was still reliant on sherry and port for cash flow.)

'Villa Maria was strong in the cream sherry business, and we would be there in the middle of winter in the dark and the cold and the rain, filling sherry drums and then loading containers to send to Wilson Neill in Dunedin,' he remembers. 'We had a big contract with them. We did sell to other wholesalers and retailers in 750ml bottles and flagons, but the bulk of it went to Wilson Neill.'

At the time, the winery's sterile filtration equipment was not as fast as the bottling line, which was packed into a converted double garage at the back of the original Fistonich house. If there was a big bottling day it meant someone had to start at 4am to fire up the boiler, sterilise the filter pads and filler, and get a head-start on the line. 'It was not a good idea to sleep in, as production was run by Kevin Blincoe and he could be quite fiery if the winery did not perform the way he thought it should,' recalls Fabian Yukich.

It took some time for Polglase to settle into his role at Villa. Keen to be part of the winemaking industry, all the same he was not expecting to be filling sherry drums in the freezing night for weeks on end, and he began to think he might have chosen the wrong vocation.

But after one of George's legendary staff parties any notion that he was in the wrong job disappeared. These were held around once a month, depending on the time of year and stage of the vintage. There were not many staff at that point, so the parties had a family feel to them. George's grape-grower neighbours — Ian Montgomerie, Ross Ellet and John Lambie — were frequently among the guests, as were many of Villa Maria's customers and suppliers. The parties followed a set format and everybody had a job. The winemaker's task was to organise a cocktail that was appropriate for the theme of the party.

'This particular party, my first, had an island theme and I think we made a piña colada,' remembers Polglase. 'It was compulsory for everyone to have a glass of this on your way in. The night began straight after work, and around 7 or 8pm the dancing started, with music provided by this group of local Islanders who came in, and Rob Skiffington, who was a one-man-band with a guitar and all these songs in this machine. It wasn't until later in the evening that the salads, cheese and French sticks with garlic butter, lamb on the spit, and chicken came out, and by this time everyone was in a very relaxed frame of mind. I thought, "What a great night — this makes all the miserable night-work worthwhile!"'

In fact, looking after staff was always high on George's agenda. 'There was always plenty of ti-tree wood around the vineyard, and after a long shift we would frequently light a fire and have a late-night barbecue. I guess it was partly to do with the Croatian desire to be good hosts and good employers,' he says. Not content with simply playing host at his parties, George was also a dab-hand on the barbecue, something that impressed guests at the functions he would hold for visitors to the winery, events that often included more than one notable wine writer.

'We would cut six 44-gallon drums in half, and could feed up to 600 people at trade days,' he remembers. 'I could line up and cook 100 steaks on my own. Then when these events got bigger I organised all the staff, including sale reps and marketing managers, and taught them how to cook a decent steak. I actually became quite well-known for my cooking skills.'

The winery built by George in 1969 was not only used for staff parties and trade functions and as the venue for the first Villa Maria: Living With Wine Club; for many years it was also hired out to local

George with Mark Polglase,
at left, Harry Wright and a
new line in cask wine.

clubs for functions, and was used as a venue for family celebrations such as weddings. George had employed a full-time caterer, Brian Meads, and he would ensure the guests were always well-fed.

IT WAS ASSUMED that Mike Bennett would eventually take over from Harry Wright, but it seems Bennett had other ideas. In 1979 Bennett left Villa for Te Mata Vineyards in Hawke's Bay, taking with him an English girl who worked in the Villa Maria office and whom he later married. (Bennett was to stay at Te Mata until 1985, when he and Martin Elliott established the small Havelock North winery St George.) Bennett's unexpected departure meant that Mark Polglase was appointed assistant winemaker.

Wright and Polglase made a good team, but George, then as now, was never far from the action. 'In terms of what got apportioned to which wine, George would decide. Each day he would make a point of having a catch-up to see what was going well and what needed attention,' says Polglase. George was involved in tasting the base wines, and would be present when decisions were made regarding the eventual blend destined for consumers. In the event of any indecision, the winemaking team would submit blends of what they thought worked best for George to taste, and then he would make any adjustments he thought necessary.

Harry Wright was experienced and knowledgeable in both viticulture and winemaking. Over time Polglase, with his academic background, contributed scientific rigour and technique, as well as new ideas, to the mix. On Polglase's watch, barrel fermentation and lees stirring were introduced, and George credits him with being one of the early adopters in New Zealand of these techniques. At the same time, rigorous monitoring of ferments, cork-quality checks and anaerobic winemaking techniques were adopted as essential winemaking practices at Villa.

The Villa Maria policy of using dry ice to reduce as much as possible any opportunity for the wine to come in contact with air from the time it was in the tanker until it was bottled set them apart from their competitors. The winemakers at Villa had introduced 'snowdroppers' into the bottling line, which would dispense a small packet of dry ice into the bottle before it was filled. As soon as the wine hit the bottom of the bottle and came in contact with the dry ice, a layer of gas would form, preventing the wine coming into contact with the air.

'I don't know if anyone else was doing that in New Zealand but we certainly were among the first, if not the first, to introduce it on any scale,' says Polglase.

Polglase and Wright were also brought into regular brainstorming discussions with Warwick Orchiston at Vidal, but had little if anything to do with the wine styles he produced. The company policy was that each winemaker was in charge of his own wines.

The vineyards around Kirkbride Road were looked after by Morrie Reeves, who was already in his sixties when Polglase joined Villa. When Reeves retired in 1984 George hired Don Gillanders, who had completed a Diploma of Agriculture. Gillanders came from a well-known South Island family in Darfield, and had been expected to join his brothers in farming. But he had married a nurse who much preferred living in the city and being able to visit restaurants, so they came to Auckland, where Polglase says he was really glad to find a job that combined his love of the land with his wife's preference for city living.

10
MARKET
RESEARCH

Villa Maria Estate

The Cabernet Sauvignon grape is used to produce most of the worlds superior Clarets. The small blue black thick skinned grapes hang in loose bunches from semi-vigorous vines. Cabernet wines possess a strong fruit flavour and bouquet and are high in acid and tannin. This Cabernet has been matured in small oak casks followed by bottle age. The wine has a full rich flavour and yet is quite delicate. It is complex with plenty of finesse. The wine will develop further with more bottle age. Recommended for cellaring. Store lying down.

SILVER AWARD
EASTER SHOW 1977

Private Bin '76
Cabernet
Sauvignon

VILLA MARIA WINES LTD. KIRKBRIDE RD. MANGERE
CONTENTS 750ml ALC. CONT.

Despite all the clever promotion, the company's domination at wine awards, and its success at developing relationships that drove sales deals, in the late 1970s Villa Maria wine sales started to dive. George couldn't understand why.

On the recommendation of John Buck he contacted Steve Bridges, who was a Reader in Marketing at Massey University in Palmerston North.

George told Bridges he was at a loss to explain the poorer-than-expected sales. He felt wine quality was not the issue, relationships with customers continued to be strong, and there were no obvious reasons the formula he had developed for growth should not be working.

Bridges was no stranger to the vicissitudes of the New Zealand wine industry. Between 1972 and 1975 he had established the marketing department at New Zealand Wines and Spirits, the company run by Lion Breweries magnate Douglas Myers and where John Buck also worked. Bridges's curiosity was piqued enough by George's approach that he took up George's offer to meet at the winery during his next visit to Auckland.

Over a period of weeks Bridges would fly to Auckland from Palmerston North and stay at George and Gail Fistonich's Epsom home. He and George would stay up late, talking, drinking wine and smoking cigarettes. Then they would get up early to start meetings at 7.30am. During their long, wide-ranging discussions, George suggested that Bridges consider developing a training programme for the sales team that could help arrest the sales slide. Bridges agreed, but he also convinced George that in order to discover if there was anything more deep-seated involved they should carry out specific market research to determine exactly what the public perception of the Villa brand was.

ESTATE BOTTLED

Villa Maria Estate

Dry White '74

A Dry White Table Wine • Chill Before Serving

VILLA MARIA WINES LTD. KIRKBRIDE RD, MANGERE AUCKLAND, N.Z.
CONTENTS 750ml ALC. CONT. 11.5% BY VOL. APPROX.

An early 'Old Masters' label.

With the help of Dr Wayne Cartwright, then Professor of Marketing at Massey University, Bridges initiated a series of four focus groups, two in Palmerston North and two in Auckland. The groups canvassed the opinions of what Bridges called 'wine enthusiasts'. First, they served the participants Villa Maria wines in unmarked carafes (to eliminate any bias). The response was universal approval of the wines. The next step was to gauge perceptions of the products of other well-known wine producers.

The participants were asked what they thought of Villa Maria and various competitive brands, including Montana, Cooks and McWilliam's. The reaction was a shock: each of the brands was viewed positively by the majority in each of the four groups, but there was a small, but significant and vocal group who voiced the opinion that Villa Maria produced 'commercial wine' at the low end of the price and quality spectrum. One even more outspoken participant described Villa Maria as the company that 'produces mass-market quaffing wine for the non-discerning wine drinker'. When Bridges began to explore the reasons for such a disconnect, Villa Maria's labels were quickly identified as an issue. Potential buyers associated the 'Old Masters' painting style of the labels with the cheap-and-nasty plonk wines of New Zealand's recent wine past.

Usually keen to make changes, George was not totally convinced that this was the heart of the problem. 'They were probably looking a bit tired, but I didn't think it was that bad,' he recalls. 'However, Steve was sure that changing the label would modernise us, and he brought in a designer, Dennis Robinson, to drastically update our image. I really couldn't think of any strong reason not to. Based on Steve's brief, the designer came up with a label with a prominent red V sitting above a stylised wine-award medallion.'

The new labels — whose dominant red 'V' and non-traditional look met with strong opposition from management and George's fellow directors — resulted in an immediate and sustained increase in sales.

'We also very nearly didn't do it because it involved a fairly major financial investment, and my financial advisor Avon Carpenter wasn't convinced it was really necessary,' says George. 'We had big debates,

The 'Old Masters' labels
were eventually shown
to be damaging the
perception of the brand.

but I had great faith in Dennis Robinson's design ability so we went ahead. That change convinced me of the need to make sure our brand is always prominent on the shelves. In some ways it confirmed us as a serious player in the wine industry. I was relieved it was a label problem and not a wine problem.' And the re-badge had another, enduring, impact. As Bridges sees it, 'the label-change exercise initiated in George a real appreciation of the importance of marketing that grew to become as important to him as commitment to quality production'.

George agrees. 'Up until this time our limited marketing budgets required an innovative approach to promotion and marketing. I had been relying on a fairly simple approach to sales and marketing, such as in-store wine tastings. All the other major players had big budgets to spend on sales and promotion. I didn't have the money to do that, and instead had to rely on my sales staff having good relationships with customers and getting as much bang for my buck as I could. I also knew that the wine-buying public was reasonably naïve about how to make good choices, so if I could give them a reason to buy my wines then I had something to work with. At that time the industry was just getting into the habit of shouting about wine awards, so it stood to reason in my mind that if I could get the awards then the retailers would tell people and the customers would know that they could rely on the Villa brand. The goal was clear: to become New Zealand's most awarded winery. This developed into the major cornerstone of Villa Maria's future. We decided we did not want to grow into a major corporate-style wine company — we would just focus on quality at all levels. This philosophy came to guide many future decisions that the company made.'

Bridges' counsel did not stop at using publicity gained through awards as a sales tool. Market research, he argued, had shown that consumers actually enjoyed the taste of Villa's wine. Now, more of them just needed to be able to access it. He developed a three-pronged strategy, with a nationwide programme of in-store wine tastings and more creative merchandising at its heart. He also convinced George, who was already a convert to the value of wine awards, to trumpet each and every success through the print media.

It was a strategy tailor-made for the company's limited marketing capacity and its budget constraints. Going for what marketers call 'below-the-line' promotion was the only way Villa Maria could compete with the big corporates who had the resources to work through high-charging advertising agencies. Precious marketing budgets could be spent on the constant training of the sales force and reinforcing in-store activity, instead of relying on high-cost advertising campaigns. The goal was that New Zealand wine consumers would see Villa Maria as a company that made quality wine. This strategy of tastings, endorsement and the management of public perception has remained at the heart of Villa Maria's marketing.

Bridges' plan bore fruit and was vindicated within months. By this time George was convinced that theirs was a valuable partnership, so when Bridges told George that the relationship between Villa Maria and pirate radio station Radio Hauraki created the wrong image, Gail says that George listened. 'George had been very involved with Hauraki for a number of years, and they were always playing this slogan "Let Villa Maria introduce you to wine",' she says. 'Villa wine was always served at Radio Hauraki parties and functions. Then one night there was a big party on board their boat *Tiri* to celebrate their last night as an illegal "pirate" station, because the government had finally given them a broadcasting licence. Unfortunately during the night one of the DJs fell overboard and drowned. In the *Herald* the next morning they had a picture of the guys on the boat and they were holding a bottle of Villa Maria.' It wasn't the type of publicity Villa Maria needed.

Another change in George's promotions strategy occurred around the same time. 'The wine-and-cheese parties we were sponsoring had actually got a bit out of hand. They were really popular and dozens of people would turn up, but things would quickly become very raucous. People were not really used to drinking wine in those days, and some would overdo it, go home with major headaches, and next morning decide they would never drink Villa Maria wine again. In a way our generosity was becoming counter-productive, so we scaled back.'

HAWKES BAY
Riesling~Sylvaner
1982

A premium dry white wine showing the distinctive
fruit character of the Riesling Sylvaner grape,
a variety that flourishes in the fertile
'fruitbowl' area of New Zealand's
Hawkes Bay province.
Serve slightly
chilled.

VILLA MARIA

Made and bottled on the Villa Maria Estate

VILLA MARIA WINES LTD AUCKLAND NZ ALC CONT 10.5% BY VOL 750ml

The bold red 'V' design that has
been the Villa Maria badge, with
slight tweaks and refinements,
since the early 1980s.

IN 1987 STEVE Bridges left Massey University to set up his own marketing consultancy in Auckland. When George was short of a marketing manager, Bridges stepped into the breach for just over a year while George found a replacement. George has involved him as a consultant ever since. He remains involved in the Villa Maria sales and marketing staff training, undertakes research projects, critiques the drafts of all the company's marketing communication materials, and has developed the company's merchandising training scheme. Bridges, quite possibly more than anyone else in the history of Villa Maria, has George Fistonich's ear. As Bridges puts it, 'George calls me whenever he has an idea about something.'

In 1983 the Fistonich/Bridges partnership made headlines. Bridges had persuaded George to adopt an advertising campaign involving 'positioning', an aggressive marketing concept that was at the time popular in the United States. 'This is based on the premise that consumers can usually only recall three or four brands in a product category, so you have to ensure your brand is among the three to four that are remembered,' Bridges explains. 'You position your brand through a direct comparison to the larger and more successful brands, and leverage off the recognition that results from association. For example, a soft drink called 7Up was positioned as "uncola" — obviously leveraging off Coca Cola — and Avis positioned itself against Hertz as "We try harder; we're #2". It's a great way for smaller players to gain a place beside the market leaders. You look for ways to link your brand with theirs and lead people to see you as a part of the leader group.'

Under Bridges' direction, a series of magazine advertisements was developed that showed bottles of Villa Maria wines standing beside bottles of Montana wines. At the time Montana was the best-known brand in the country and held around 33 per cent of the market. The text accompanying the images implied that Villa Maria was as good as Montana, and that consumers had a choice between two equally strong brands. In short, they didn't have to choose Montana to be drinking the market leader. 'At no time did we slag off Montana,' says Bridges. 'In fact, the ads were intentionally complimentary

Which one did you choose last night?

These two popular medium white wines share one thing in common. They're both premium wines. Brookvale, with its fruity fresh after-taste is certainly Villa Maria's most popular wine.

Blenheimer, with its fruity Moselle style is undoubtedly Montana's most sought-after wine.

Both are medal winners.

What is it that these two great winemakers attribute to the popularity of their wines?

There can only be one answer. Personal preference.

VILLA MARIA
WINNING WINES

GNA 1129

One of the advertisements
that landed Villa Maria before
a High Court judge.

about Montana, because we wanted to position Villa Maria alongside a successful brand.'

Montana took exception. Within days, court action was taken, Montana's lawyers claiming that the ads left the impression that they were placed jointly by Villa Maria and Montana, and were therefore misleading.

Ultimately the High Court ruled in favour of Montana, forbidding Villa Maria from continuing its campaign. Villa Maria then went to the Court of Appeal, which overturned the High Court decision and lifted the injunction. Montana then threatened to take Villa Maria to the Privy Council, at which time George, with no money to fight that particular battle, agreed to remove the ads.

The print media followed the court battle every step of the way. High-profile Auckland legal firms were involved, with Buddle Weir and Co acting for Montana and Webster Malcolm Kirkpatrick QC acting for Villa Maria.

Although Villa Maria couldn't afford to go all the way to the Privy Council, the company gained benefit from the legal battle. 'It was great publicity,' remembers George, 'and once again placed Villa Maria top-of-mind with consumers. Most importantly, the effect of the ads lasted a very long time due to the long life of magazines in homes, hair salons and doctors' surgeries all over the country.'

In the game of positioning, of winning the hearts and minds of the public, the campaign was masterfully played.

11
AUSTRALIA, ASIA AND BEYOND

By the late 1970s, the development of the new winery, the purchase of Vidal, and the extra costs associated with marketing and promotion were straining Villa Maria's finances. The situation was exacerbated by growing competition. Villa Maria's financial controller, John Hollows, felt the company was too stretched and recommended that George engage Tauranga lawyer and professional director Avon Carpenter to make some recommendations.

George leads a wine
tasting for sales staff at
the winery.

One of the first suggestions Carpenter made was that George develop a more formal management structure, and as a result in 1980 he and Steve Bridges became the first formal directors of Villa Maria Wines.

Despite the financial strain imposed by growth, as the 1970s turned into the 1980s Villa Maria was in good shape. The company had high-quality contracts with grape growers, sales were consistent and growing, and there was further expansion, particularly in the Hawke's Bay. George was in good spirits. He instituted management reforms, establishing the first formal set of company standards and beginning to bed in the notion of what he called 'quality, quality, quality'. The company increased its focus on training sales staff and began to look more seriously at the export market.

Around George, however, the very nature of the wine industry was changing. The camaraderie that had characterised the earlier years was being replaced by bitterness and rivalry brought about by rapid expansion, intense competition, and the involvement of large corporate entities. The bigger players would give no quarter to the small family-owned and -operated enterprises that had been responsible for bringing wine to the attention of the New Zealand consumer.

Then in the late 1970s the wine industry was embarrassed by the publication of a series of scientific studies that showed that some producers were guilty of adding water to their table wines to 'stretch' the quantities to meet growing demand. Although the practice was historic and illegal, some winemakers were using it to reduce the acidity and ameliorate the unwanted flavours often found in wine made from hybrid grapes and sold mainly in cask form — so-called 'flavoured wine'.

Quality-oriented winemakers were keen that there be legislation to end the practice, and some time later the government amended the food and drug regulations to do away entirely with the flavoured-wine category. Drafted with the support of grape growers and winemakers, new regulations set a minimum of grape juice in all table wines. The industry was given a probation period of 18 months, or two vintages, to tidy itself up. 'There's little doubt that the modern New Zealand wine industry is now one of the best self-regulated wine industries in the world,' says George.

Villa Maria was not troubled by the scandal or the legislative changes; its reputation was unsullied. In fact, Villa Maria's Camberley Dry was used as a benchmark by John Dunbar, the Waikato University master's student who had developed the oxygen isotope method that could be used to determine whether water in wine (or any other drink) was natural water from the grape fruit or added tap water.

During this period, Villa Maria's rapid growth and competition success substantially increased its attractiveness to investors looking for opportunities to enter the wine market. George would get regular approaches to see if he would sell. There were regular invitations to lunch, where the notion would be broached. Callers were wasting their time. As he puts it, 'I haven't voluntarily given my books to anyone in my life.'

He had plenty to occupy himself with otherwise. The race for market share was heating up dramatically. Many smaller producers began to struggle financially when a surge in import volumes hit local wine producers' margins, which were already being pinched by consumer price-resistance. At the same time, the bigger producers were in a race to plant new vineyards. There was plenty of incentive to do so: the Wine Industry Development Plan had predicted a growth in consumption, and the government was offering tax incentives to encourage development of a range of products, including wine.

In 1984, sales tax on fortified wines (ports and sherries) was lifted by 54 per cent and on table wine by 83 per cent. These were not the conditions for growth, and companies with excess wine began to strategise about how to reduce stocks.

The winemaking community was extremely angry about the increase, and George agreed to host a meeting in the Villa Maria boardroom between 20 winemakers, Prime Minister David Lange, who was also Fistonich's local MP, and finance minister Roger Douglas. Most of the members of the older Auckland Croatian winemaking fraternity were there — Mate Selak, Mate Brajkovich, Tony Soljan and Peter Babich among them — and the mood was dark. There was no doubt that Lange and Douglas were going to get a very thorough going-over.

Lange arrived first, bursting into the room and then striding to the window to look out at the cars parked below. 'My word, you guys must be doing so well,' George remembers him saying. 'Mercedes, BMWs, Audis, Range Rovers . . . Congratulations!'

'I see Douglas is not here,' Lange went on, 'but when he arrives, give him hell.' Then, says George, Lange went to the table and grabbed himself a sausage roll and sat down as if to say 'This could be interesting'. 'I've never seen the mood in a room change so quickly — he completely disarmed us all. When Douglas did arrive, a more reasonable conversation took place than we'd all planned. It was a great example of Lange's extraordinary use of personality and humour to control a room.'

IN SEPTEMBER 1982 George had approached Ian Clark, a man with a long association with the wine and spirits business, and asked him to join Villa Maria as public relations manager. He told Clark that he wanted to change the direction of Villa Maria by increasing its exposure to the market, and that he wanted Clark to be the public face of the company. Clark was somewhat taken aback by this. 'George had a very strong profile in the wine community, but not many outside of that knew him well. I had heard him give sales presentations where he was very confident, but I had also seen a more retiring side in social situations which involved large numbers of people.'

At the time Clark was working at Mission Vineyards in Napier, and was responsible for re-developing the company and restoring the status it had once held. It was a good job, and Clark felt there was still more he could do there. But George's offer appealed, and there was the family to consider. Clark told George that he would consult with his wife, as any move to Auckland would have major implications for her and their seven children. As it turned out they decided it was a good time to make a move, as their oldest child was about to start secondary school.

Clark started work at Kirkbride Road in February 1983, officially as public relations manager, but he was much more than that behind the scenes. Appreciative of Clark's broad knowledge of the industry, George would often use him as a sounding board for his plans and schemes. Clark's close connections with grape growers, especially in Hawke's Bay, would also prove to be hugely beneficial in an era when the supply of grapes was still short, and sometimes George would involve him in meetings with suppliers and growers.

Initially Clark's primary task was to ensure that the Villa Maria brand received plenty of attention from wine writers, general media and customers. Steve Bridges and George had a plan to use competition results as a primary way of creating consumer awareness of Villa Maria. 'Villa spent bugger-all on advertising, so we had to make use of all the publicity we could that came from sponsorship of events and the arts and from success at wine awards,' says Clark. Fortunately, the awards were coming in thick and fast.

'George used to tell the new staff, especially during the orientation we give them when they start working here, that he used to be the winemaker, and that back in 1963, at the Easter Show, Villa Maria Burgundy and a red table wine won second and third prizes,' says Clark. 'Of course they did not have gold and silver medals in those days. But when George really started to get results was in 1979, when all the new vineyards were coming on-stream, particularly in Gisborne and the Hawke's Bay. That was the year when all the wines we entered, except one, won an award at the New Zealand Trade and Industry Wine Show — later to become the Air New Zealand Wine Awards. It was an unprecedented haul. Steve Bridges designed a half-page advertisement that said all these wines had won an award and also made a feature of the one wine that did not receive an award. It was really effective and set the tone of how we publicised our success from that point on. And it kept me very busy.'

When Clark joined Villa Maria, New Zealand wine exports were growing but were still at very low levels. Only the large producers were sending any significant quantities of wine overseas, and at nowhere near the level they would achieve later in the decade. Indeed, the country was still a net importer of wine. Small parcels of Villa wines were being sent to Taiwan, Tahiti and to the American Army base in the Philippines, but this was on an ad-hoc basis. The company was in essence, as wine writer Michael Cooper put it, 'a conspicuous absentee from the large group of winemakers which swung into export in the mid-1980s'.

Export had always been high on the agenda for George. 'We all knew export was critical to our survival. When Avon Carpenter came on board he insisted that we should be looking at the Asia market, which was where some of the other companies had gone. So in 1979 my sales manager Bill Bruce and I went and spent a few weeks looking at Singapore, Hong Kong, Japan, Vietnam and Thailand. I remember seeing Montana's White Hermitage gathering dust on shelves around Asia, and I thought going in there was premature. I felt that we were about 10 years too early. I didn't believe we were ready to make our mark in export. We needed to further improve our vineyards and varieties, and we needed to develop more international marketing and packaging. We needed to take a long-term view.' He returned from Asia and went back to focusing on growing new varietals.

Around 1984, John Taylor MW and an associate from the British company Grants of St James, whose subsidiary, Hatch Mansfield, specialised in fine wines, visited George at Villa to see whether they could distribute Villa Maria wines in the United Kingdom. George was tempted, but he still felt that although the wine quality was up to the mark, the packaging was not up to international standards. He did not take up the opportunity.

In 1985 George sent Clark and Steve Bridges to View '85, a large wine expo in Melbourne, Australia. The idea was to have a look at the market and to identify any barriers to entry as well as any potential opportunities. During the trip they identified the well-known and highly regarded distributor Tucker Seabrook as the ideal company to represent Villa Maria. However, Tucker Seabrook had the distribution agency for Cloudy Bay and could not free itself up to take on Villa Maria.

At the time Australia was producing substantial quantities of its own wine and was importing only around 4000 cases of wine per year, most of it sweet German wines such as Blue Nun, Liebfraumilch and Mateus Rosé. Consumer support for these brands and for Australian wines was so strong that there was little interest in anything from New Zealand. Clark and Bridges returned to New Zealand and briefed George on the situation.

George made the decision to wait for a good national distributor before totally committing to that market. It was not until 2003, when the distributor Tucker Seabrook lost Cloudy Bay as part of a restructure and approached Villa Maria as their ideal substitute for Cloudy Bay, that Villa Maria wines finally entered the Australian market with a national distributor.

This did not mean that the idea of exporting Villa wine was entirely shelved, however. In 1986 overseas markets were once again identified as holding the key to Villa Maria's future growth and success. As Clark was to play a pivotal role in making this happen, in that year in addition to his PR role he was appointed export manager. Again, various markets were explored as options, and this time the United Kingdom was identified as being a market of promise.

So it was that on 14 October 1988 the first consignment of Villa Maria wines was sent to the United Kingdom. Computer technology was only just coming on-stream at the time, but Clark has handwritten records that detail the shipment.

'This decision to export to the United Kingdom further delayed taking on the Australian market,' explains Clark. 'The real issue was that good New Zealand wine was in comparatively short supply up until 2008, and we, like others, were in no position to supply every market. The last thing we wanted was to go into a market and then not to be able to supply. As it was, we struggled to meet demand in the UK, and we didn't want to have wine on the shelves for three months of the year and then nothing for the other nine months. That would really get the retailers annoyed and we would end up being de-listed. So we decided to just drip-feed Australia when we could.'

In 1992 Villa Maria began exporting into sectors of the Asian market through a company called North East Trading, but once again quantities were very small. In 1992 George travelled to Hong Kong to launch his wines, and in 1996 an importer in the United States, Vineyard Brands Inc, showed an interest in stocking Villa Maria. Exports of Villa Maria to the United States had begun.

'The budgeted 8000 cases snowballed to 30,000 cases, and so we were quickly out of stock and had to delay our entry to Australia,' says George. Today exports account for approximately 70 per cent of Villa Maria's sales by volume.

THE FANTASTIC VILLA Maria wines of the 1985 vintage were the last to be made for George by Mark Polglase, who, once vintage was complete in September 1985, left the company after eight-and-a-half years to join Penfolds New Zealand, which had been sold by Frank Yukich in 1982 to Lion Breweries.

'I felt this was a good time to go,' he says. 'The 1985 vintage had been good for Villa. We had a really good crew, and it was a big year in terms of the sheer volume that came on-stream. Every single tank of wine I left behind in 1985 was like, wow! And that helped no end, because later in the year George was sitting on a stock of really good wines that he was able to sell at the top end.'

'I just felt I had learnt everything about how wine was made at Villa,' Polglase says of his reasons for leaving the company. 'I felt I could progress more if I saw how others were doing it. Soon after

I left I had a chance to see what other wineries were doing. In the mid-1980s the winemaking techniques at Villa, with its innovative quality control systems, its attention to detail, and anaerobic wine-making, certainly compared favourably with many companies — and in many cases were 10 years ahead of anyone else.' (Polglase rejoined Villa Maria in November 2009, and has been in charge of the cellar door there since then.)

In other words, George's drive for quality, quality, quality was bearing fruit. However, by the early 1980s he knew he had to build up the expertise of his winemaking staff. Following the resignation of assistant winemaker Patrick Brookman in September 1983, he placed advertisements in newspapers and magazines in New Zealand and Australia and received a number of replies. George and Mark Polglase travelled to Australia, where they interviewed around 60 applicants, including a number of Roseworthy College students who had been recommended by the highly regarded head of the college, Dr Bryce Rankin. Australians who had passed the Bachelor of Applied Science from Roseworthy were having an impact on the New Zealand wine industry, hence the motivation for going to the source to recruit others.

None of the initial 60 interviewed satisfied George as leading-edge quality winemakers, but 21-year-old Australian Kate Berryman (now Radburnd) impressed George enough that he offered her a job as an assistant winemaker. Although George didn't know it, Berryman was the girlfriend of a fellow student, New Zealander Brent Marris, who would himself go on to be a high-profile winemaker.

Radburnd says that working for George was a great introduction to any job. 'There was the automatic assumption that everyone would work hard, but there was also equally the opportunity to have fun, a philosophy which worked very well. We were encouraged to challenge and to question, and we were expected to stand by our opinions. George made sure relationships with co-workers, growers, the trade, media and consumers were developed and nurtured, and their importance never under-estimated. There was complete immersion in all aspects of the winery business — winemaking, grower liaison, marketing and public relations — the work environment was always inclusive. We participated with the sales team sometimes in workshops, many times in wine training, and were always made aware of market conditions through many hours spent in-market.'

After an initial introduction to the company in Auckland, Radburnd moved to the Hawke's Bay, to take up the position of assistant winemaker at Vidal under Warwick Orchiston for the 1984 and 1985 vintages. In 1985 she married Brent Marris and moved back to Auckland to become night winemaker for Villa Maria's 1986 vintage. In 1987 George appointed the now 24-year-old Radburnd to succeed Orchiston in what might have seemed a risky decision to some in the industry. But George was certain it was a safe move. (Radburnd would commute to Vidal weekly from Auckland for about a year before moving permanently to Hawke's Bay.)

'Kate was not only an excellent winemaker — particularly of Bordeaux reds — she was also a very good team player and one of the best communicators we have ever had at Villa,' remembers George. 'It was a no-brainer to have her take over when Warwick left. She gave us her total commitment.'

Radburnd, now managing director of CJ Pask Wines, is highly complimentary about George's willingness to provide the tools necessary for her to do her job, and says her 30-year winemaking career has been greatly influenced by George and his management style. 'Not only did he provide the environment to make great wine, he made sure we had the resources: winemaking equipment, new oak barrels, study tours and education. In addition he had an absolute belief that the winemaking team would achieve whatever we set out to do. We were all singular about quality, we experimented, tasted and exchanged information, all encouraged and endorsed by George. I have immense respect for this man who gave me my first job, developed my love of wine and of this challenging industry. He was a terrific role model, and I certainly hope that I have taken some of his traits and used them wisely in our winery.'

Radburnd would stay until 1990, to be succeeded by Elise Montgomery.

George and Kym Milne with a
trophy haul from the Air New
Zealand Easter Show wine awards

Grant Edmonds with his
Easter Show Wine Awards.

A SHORT WHILE after returning from Australia, George had received an application in the mail from Kym Milne, a young winemaker who had studied at Roseworthy and was working at the Consolidated Co-operative Wineries in South Australia under Ian McKenzie, their chief winemaker. McKenzie had given Milne a glowing reference, even though it was clear he really didn't want to lose his star protégé. Milne also came highly recommended by John Hancock, who was winemaker at Delegat's at the time.

George was impressed with Milne's application and the accompanying recommendations, and in December 1983 he paid $800 for Milne to fly to New Zealand for an interview. After the interview, George and Gail took Milne and Alan O'Sullivan (then a young accountant at Villa Maria and now the company secretary) to dinner at Tony's Restaurant, where George's friend Paul White was chef. The next day Mark Polglase interviewed Milne, and reported back that he was impressed. When Milne accepted George's offer to be assistant winemaker, reporting to Polglase, he became the first trained winemaker since Ross Spence to join the company.

Milne had come from a big bulk winery in South Australia, but this did not mean that the much smaller Villa Maria had nothing to teach him. He would find the company innovative and progressive; there was plenty to test him and inspire him. He worked alongside Polglase on the 1984 and 1985 vintages, and when Polglase left Villa Maria for Penfolds he took over as senior winemaker in Auckland.

Polglase was very aware of the high regard in which George held his assistant Kym Milne, and he knew that Kym, who was looking after the night wine shift, was keen to have his job. So Polglase didn't feel he would be leaving George at a loss.

It was a golden opportunity for Milne, who was only 26 years old. And the preconditions for making a positive impression were certainly good. 'We had a brilliant vintage in 1985,' he remembers. 'The weather was good, and we had an unusually large vintage and a massive supply of grapes available. This very nearly worked against us. We couldn't waste the juice, so we kept making the wine. After fermentation we had to store a lot off-site without refrigeration, and it was extremely hard. The very old racking system with the barrels permanently locked into a wooden frame that was very difficult to work with'. A positive attitude and good company culture got everyone through. 'Then of course George had to find ways to sell it.'

In the latter half of 1985 George was spending a great deal of his time dealing with banks, unhappy growers, and the continuing price war, so Milne was pretty much left to run the winery as he chose. George's instructions to him, however, were unequivocal: to make the best wine he could make.

'I was to tell him what I needed to do the job, and he would try to make sure it happened. This was an unusual but really wonderful place for any young winemaker to be in. Many of the crew at that stage were young and enthusiastic. We got on well, and we spent pretty much all our waking moments in the winery. George saw our commitment and was always happy to put on a barbecue for us in the winery as his way of recognising the effort we were putting in.'

ON THE WINEMAKING front the company was surging ahead. 1986 was another good vintage, and Villa was yet again raking in the awards, including the Air New Zealand Trophy for the 1986 Gisborne Barrique Fermented Chardonnay from the Lewis Vineyard in Gisborne. Milne credits much of this success to the good work viticulturist Debbie Reid was doing. She was, according to Milne, 'an absolute champion in the vineyards and with growers'.

It was about this time that Grant Edmonds arrived at Villa Maria. Edmonds had begun as a cellar hand in Auckland, and after vintage that year he was to work in the laboratory. Recognising his potential, George and Kym Milne sent Edmonds off to Roseworthy in 1988, before bringing him back to Auckland and a role as assistant winemaker at the end of that year.

A year later, when Tony Hooper left Esk Valley, George and Milne would turn to Edmonds to fill the gap as winemaker. He then would take cellar hand Gordon Russell with him. Edmonds worked with George for eight-and-a-half years, until leaving to co-found Redmetal Vineyards in Hawke's Bay. He told *Metro*'s Geraldine Johns in 2000 that George 'was the only employer I'd ever had who gave me the opportunity to grow'.

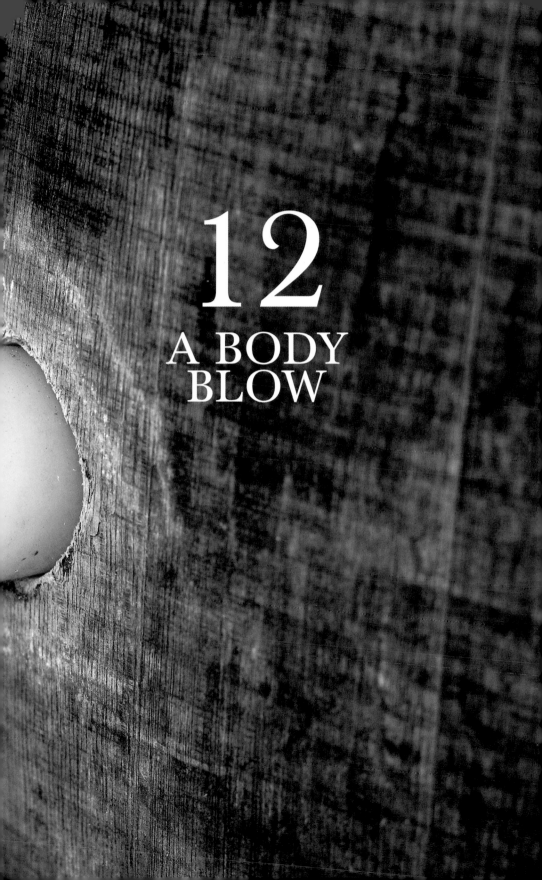

12
A BODY
BLOW

A winemaking success the company indubitably was, but by late 1985 Villa Maria was $4 million in debt and things were not looking good.

Like others in the early 1980s, Villa had experienced significant growth but low profits. Strong sales of predominantly cask wine had ensured survival. The company had wine in stock, but going into late 1984 and early 1985, the savage price war left margins extremely tight; profit was becoming even harder to come by.

George with Mangere MP
and newly elected Prime
Minister David Lange
at the winery.

P art of the reason was the fierce competition for share of grape supply, caused by new entrants to the industry. It was forcing winemakers into agreeing to ultimately untenable contracts with growers, including there being no limits to the tonnage per hectare that may have to be paid for. It was also the outcome of a price war being driven by Brierley-owned wine companies. With an eye on the expansion and rationalisation of the wine industry, Brierley Investments Limited (BIL) had purchased three of the country's major wine producers: McWilliam's, Corbans and relative newcomer Cooks Wines.

BIL's asset-stripping reputation was well-known, and many in the wine industry believed that BIL was driven by a view that there was room in New Zealand for only two major wine producers. Most felt that BIL had no real understanding of how the wine industry worked, of how long it took to realise a profit, and of the trends in consumer wine preference.

'In its typically aggressive way the company began to try to create problems for smaller players by squeezing margins, and dumping large quantities of wine into the market, and by taking prices down to unsustainable levels,' says George. 'The total market was so small that it was incredibly sensitive to any fluctuations in volume or price, and most companies had to follow the market down.'

It was almost a perfect storm: a large quantity of Marlborough

Sauvignon Blanc coming onto the market, many new companies starting up, established producers experiencing significant growth, grape production increasing, imports growing, and consumer price-resistance building. The only antidote to that could be a sharp increase in wine-consumption levels; consumption *was* increasing, but not quickly enough to provide any sort of salvation.

It wasn't as though no one had noticed the storm building. As Michael Cooper puts it in his *Wine Atlas of New Zealand*, 'Heavy planting of new vineyards in the 1980s — encouraged by distortionary tax incentives then offered to many land-based products — raised the spectre of a wine glut.' The 1985 grape crop was the biggest ever, a production increase of 43 per cent; Cooper called it a surplus 'of record proportions'. Its like would not be experienced again until 2008.

A small number of larger companies, including those involved in the vicious pricing battle, united to convince the government that there were in fact too many smaller producers growing inferior grapes, and that this was placing the industry under threat. George remembers the debate well. 'At one point there was a wine growers' meeting at Montana. A number of smaller wine companies arrived to see Roger Douglas, who was Minister of Finance at the time, leaving. There clearly had been some lobbying going on between the big guys, Douglas and the Prime Minister David Lange, who, as it happens, was my local Member of Parliament. Obviously it had worked.'

In 1986 the government agreed to provide a financial incentive of $6175 per hectare to growers to pull out their vines, thus reducing the quantity of grapes available by 25 per cent. Many growers — especially those who supplied smaller wineries and those already facing financial pressure — took up the offer, and in excess of 1500 hectares was stripped of vines.

The most heavily affected regions were Gisborne (586 hectares) and Hawke's Bay (534 hectares), and the variety that suffered most was Müller Thurgau (507 hectares). 'The irony of the situation was that the excess grape supply was actually caused by the big corporates, such as Cooks, which with rapid growth as its goal had initiated the expansionary planting of grapes that was not matched by an equivalent growth in market share and investment.

'Most, not all, of the smaller companies and some of the larger companies were actually managing the planting of grapes very well, and were much more aware of what varieties were required to meet the needs of their market share and their own growth, which was much more incremental,' says George.

The great 'grape pull' had a silver lining. George, along with several other winemakers, had for a long time been intent on encouraging growers to move away from oversupplied varieties (such as Müller Thurgau, Palomino and Chasselas) and from unpopular hybrids (such as Seibel 5455 and 4643 and Barco 22A), and instead to plant 'vinifera' varieties (such as Chardonnay and Sauvignon Blanc) that were more suited to the premium bottled table wines he was looking to promote and grow.

The vine pull had made growers uneasy about the future; they were looking for ways of ensuring their survival, and so switching their vines to varieties which gave winemakers more flexibility seemed a sensible option. After years of tussling with them, George finally had them on board.

Like many others working for Villa Maria at the time, Debbie Gilchrist believes that first the grape pull was a blessing in disguise for the company, as it allowed it to get out of the high-volume market and accelerate its entry into the top-end quality market.

'During this period growers provided their grapes not knowing whether they would be paid,' Debbie recalls. 'The previous years' work, developing close relationships with growers, helping them to maximise the quality in their vineyards and finding an equitable method to price grapes, ensured that we had our grape supply for the next vintage.'

IF THE EXTRAORDINARY 1985 vintage compounded the supply issues that had arisen out of the previous two vintages, which had also exceeded expectations, then some companies' problems were also compounded by long-term contracts with growers — anywhere between 10 and 99 years — with the purchase price of the grapes based on a cost-plus basis, along with a bonus for grapes that had high sugar levels.

By June 1985 the discounting of wines had reached its peak. Prior to the price war, Montana had had a market share of around 33 per cent, while the Cooks/McWilliam's share was at 26 per cent. When Cooks/McWilliam's discounted its wines in an effort to move its surplus wine and make way for the new vintage, its share of market rose to 33 per cent and Montana's dropped to 26 per cent. In response, Montana discounted further. And so the war between the larger players went on.

Like many other smaller producers, including Nobilo's, Delegat's and Glenvale, George could not afford to be out of step with the prices being charged by his large corporate competitors. When prices fell still further, George began to haemorrhage money. Sales of Villa's wines were still strong, but cash flow was tight and the ability to meet debt commitments on the borrowings used to fund growth was becoming increasingly strained.

To illustrate the effect the price war was having on Villa Maria, George and Ian Clark drew a chart that compared year-on-year sales figures. In November 1984, the company was selling around 35,000 cases of wine per month (comprising cask and bottles) and was making in the region of half a million dollars in profit. The following November they sold the same amount of wine but lost half a million. In just one month Villa Maria lost $300,000 even though it sold 30,000 cases of wine, and in just over one three-week period discounting went from 20 per cent to over 65 per cent, below cost.

However, while it had debts, the company was reasonably asset-rich. It had wine stock, it had a modern 12,000-square-foot winery, and it had Vidal. It also had 100 acres in Ihumatao, Mangere (considered prime grape-growing land), under contract to growers Ian Montgomerie and John Lambie, and access to grapes from Ross Ellet, all considered to be 'friends to Villa'. In addition, George had excellent long-term vineyard contracts in Hawke's Bay, Gisborne and Te Kauwhata. These contract arrangements were potentially extremely valuable to other wine producers looking to increase their supply of fruit.

Nonetheless, even a strong asset portfolio could not help with the cash-flow problem caused by continuous low prices. Villa Maria couldn't pay the interest on its loans or meet already deferred payments to growers which should have been cleared the previous September. In addition, the company could not pay deposits to growers on the 1986 vintage.

At the time George had a financial partner, the Auckland businessman John Spencer, who had invested in Villa Maria Wines in the early 1980s. Spencer was a very reserved man who wanted his association with Villa Maria kept confidential. George had met Spencer through Villa Maria director Avon Carpenter at a time when he required a greater degree of financial stability. Spencer came in on a 50/50 shareholding, but George remained governing director.

'I felt that he had difficulty coming to terms with the volatile nature of the industry, particularly the fact that profits could be decided by the quality and size of the vintage, by the forces of nature,' says George.

'It became obvious early on that he was uncomfortable with having much less control over the return on his investment than he had with his other investments. I didn't think he showed any real interest in backing it in its current ownership and structure. He was very close to Bob Matthew of Magnum Corporation (the BIL subsidiary that owned Corbans, Cooks and McWilliam's), and I was aware of talk that BIL wanted to buy Villa Maria. Spencer knew we were up against it, but he made it clear that he would not offer any financial support to assist Villa through the cash-flow problems. Spencer's links were with the traditional banks, so that's when I began to try to find extra capital from non-traditional sources.'

George's usual funding source was the ANZ bank, but now because of the financial pressure he found himself turning to Allan Hawkins's Equiticorp, which advanced him a further $300,000 and took a second debenture over Villa Maria.

'I often wondered whether there was bad blood between Spencer and Allan Hawkins,' he says, 'because when Spencer found out he was extremely annoyed.'

There was no sign of the price war abating; indeed, it looked as though it would continue into the following year. After considerable analysis of the situation, George and Avon Carpenter decided to have confidential talks with the banks about the continuing deterioration of the industry and the possibility of running out of equity and of having to go into voluntary receivership. George felt as though his efforts to save the company were being thwarted at every turn. 'During the price war a director of Brierley's was a fairly frequent visitor to the Villa Maria offices, to have a friendly talk about the state of the industry. In mid-October I was asked by John Wadams from Staples Rodway [Spencer's alternate on the Villa board] to attend a meeting at his office in Auckland to discuss a possible solution to our financial issues. This guy was there. The tone at the beginning was reasonably friendly, and then this chap, on behalf of Brierley's, made me an offer of a million dollars for a complete buy-out of Villa, the land, building and business.

'I had anticipated that the meeting would be stressful and had gone for a long morning walk to relax and prepare my thoughts. I'd determined that I would act in a completely relaxed manner. When I totally rejected the offer, the others at the meeting became very annoyed. One of them said, "Do you realise you are completely broke and will be in receivership in a few weeks?" I was stunned. How did they know? The tone became very aggressive and the meeting ended abruptly.

'I happened to catch the same lift downstairs as this guy, who had been visiting me over the past year for friendly chats and who was now on his way to the airport. I suggested we share a cab since we were both going in the same direction. He completely ignored my offer and went off on his own.

'I thought it was an appalling display of bad manners, and it made me think what an immature bunch of people worked for some of New Zealand's most influential and important companies.'

IN THE END, the receivership forced by the ANZ in late October 1985 could not be avoided. Karen Fistonich, George's elder daughter and the current chair of Villa Maria's board, was not working at Villa at the time of the receivership, but she has clear memories of George's state of mind in the months leading up to the receivership. 'Dad was always really busy with work, but this time it was different. He was talking about the problems openly, about what the options were; he didn't want to sell, but nor did he want to be in debt. He was under lots of stress and I knew that he was trying to decide what to do. He never asked me directly, but I knew things were not good. It wasn't sudden, it seemed to build. There was a growing realisation of the issues and what needed to be done. I suppose it brought out a survival instinct in him.'

In mid-October 1985, when it appeared that total equity could well be wiped out by Christmas, Avon Carpenter suggested that George talk to the ANZ about voluntary receivership. The bank agreed that receivership was the right option, and, after discussions with John Wadams, the wheels were set in motion. The next step in the process came in late October, when the bank appointed Peter Howell, a partner with well-known accounting firm Coopers & Lybrand, as a consultant to Villa Maria. Howell's close inspection of the Villa Maria accounts showed the company to be still solvent, but when retail wine prices once again dropped — and with no prospect of them rising again before Christmas — the ANZ formally notified George of its decision to place the company in receivership around 1 November, with Howell as receiver.

George, however, was not prepared to go down without a fight. Serendipitously, that same week he had been advised that Villa Maria wines had won all three of the trophies available to New Zealand wines at the Australian Wine Awards: Best New Zealand White Table Wine, Best New Zealand Red Table Wine, and Best Table Wine overall. The results, however, were embargoed until mid-November. George, delighted, believed that this success, if promoted well, would result in substantial extra sales, generating valuable extra revenue and cash-flow. He contacted Peter Howell and requested a delay in the receivership, but was told it was unlikely. Desperate, he found the Wellington home telephone number of the chairman of the ANZ and rang him directly.

'I'd tried all options and this was my last resort. I rang him at 7pm and got the babysitter. She told me he would be back at 11pm, so I waited until then and then rang him, told him of the situation with the awards, and said that it would be irresponsible if the receivership wasn't delayed for two weeks. If it wasn't, we'd be prevented from getting very good press and better sales that would help us recover debt and pay the creditors back more quickly. Fortunately he listened and agreed, and next day we were told the receivership had been delayed until Friday, 15 November.'

George used the two-week period of grace in typical fashion, and went into campaign mode. He contacted Steve Bridges, his trusted marketing advisor, and between them they began to formulate a plan to save the company. Their overall strategy hinged on a plea to New Zealanders' sense of fair play — a David versus Goliath approach.

He called Ian Clark into his office and told him to go to Australia, collect the awards and get back to Auckland by the following Monday. George asked Bridges to work on a newspaper ad that trumpeted the awards Villa had received, and he began to contact media. The strategy was typical of George, remembers Clark. 'George always said that if you were going to do something then you had to be first. That way you would get all the benefits from any publicity.'

When Clark arrived back from the awards presentation in Canberra on the morning of Monday, 18 November, he went straight to Villa Maria and found at least one television crew and numerous members of the print media waiting. He thrust the trophies into George's hands and the cameras rolled.

The following morning *The New Zealand Herald* ran a front-page story with the headline 'Success on a sad day for winemaker'. The accompanying picture showed George with the three 'prestigious' awards.

The article turned out to be the perfect start to the campaign. There was an unprecedented deluge of commentary in newspapers

Ian Montgomerie, John Lambie and Ross Ellet were
Mangere landowners who'd converted their dairy
land to growing grapes for Villa Maria. They are
shown here with George and former Prime Minister
Rob Muldoon at an Ihumatao vineyards launch
event. At the height of the receivership crisis they
took out a full-page newspaper advertisement to
declare their support for Villa Maria.

throughout New Zealand, all of which was sympathetic to Villa Maria's plight. For example, Warren Berryman, then one of New Zealand's top investigative journalists, wrote in the *National Business Review* that 'wine distributors were united in their opinion that Villa Maria was "steamrollered flat by the Brierley-Cooks-McWilliam's combine".'

They were not the only ones to be hit by the price war. Nobilo's had to sell strategic vineyard assets (while keeping its site at Huapai), and it weakened the company's financial structure. Delegat's went into receivership a month after Villa Maria. Glenvale, in the Hawke's Bay, was in trouble but survived for another year.

IN THE DAYS immediately leading to the official appointment of the receiver, George, ever optimistic that he could prevent the receivership, had for the most part kept the seriousness of the situation from his staff. A few of the more senior staff knew, but as things rapidly progressed George knew he would have to let Villa Maria employees know what was happening and how it would affect them. He had always felt a strong obligation to his staff, and he was determined they would be dealt with in the most supportive way possible. George also knew that it was crucial to his 'Save Villa Maria' plans that he had control of the information staff were given. 'I thought it was important that they were included, and I knew that having them here in Auckland would provide an ideal opportunity to do a bit of planning — get them motivated, so they remained positive and would get out there talking to customers, telling them our side of the story.'

He persuaded the ANZ bank to allow the necessary arrangements for receivership to take place over a weekend, and then he contacted Peter Howell and told him he was going to spend company money to bring all the sales reps from around the country to Auckland so they could be informed of the situation in person. Howell worried that the bank would disapprove of the expenditure, but George persisted. He argued that it would be better in the long run and would allow for a speedier recovery and repayment of debt. Finally agreement was reached, and George arranged for staff from as far away as Dunedin

WINNING ~~CHOICE~~

No more competition
No more choice
No more winners

> "Long term this will be disastrous both for the industry and the public because there will be increasing erosion of competition, choice of product and quality will be at risk."

Just last month at the Australian Wine Show in Canberra Villa Maria won all three trophies for 'Best New Zealand Wines' – 3 'firsts' out of 109 New Zealand entries!

On the same day Villa Maria went into voluntary receivership – victim of an insane price-cutting war that now threatens to destroy New Zealands leading independent wine makers.

Villa Maria's sister company, Vidal is also in receivership.

So too, now is Delegat's.

Maybe there <u>are</u> too many grapes. Maybe there <u>are</u> advantages in being able to buy wine 50% below cost.

But there is no advantage to anyone – especially the consumer if all that survives are one or two powerful wine monopolies.

Stanley Harris President
Federation of Wine and Food Federation.

Villa Maria Wines hailed 'Best in New Zealand.'

These two wines won <u>all</u> <u>three</u> top trophies for NZ wines at the recent Australian Wine Show.
Best New Zealand red wine – 1983 Villa Maria Private Bin Pinot Noir. Best New Zealand overall wine – 1983 Villa Maria Private Bin Pinot Noir. Best New Zealand White Wine – 1984 Villa Maria Private Bin Sauvignon Blanc.

**If you like Villa Maria or Vidal Wines and you want to buy them in the future, please buy them now.
It is quite literally the only thing you can do to preserve choice.**

VILLA MARIA
WINNING WINES

VIDAL

GNAK 718

WHO SAID NO ONE CARES?

If no one had heard of Villa Maria or Vidal Wines before they went into receivership they certainly know of them now!

Public support for Villa Maria owner George Fistonich is

VILLA MARIA AND VIDAL, EVERYONE'S TALKING ABOUT YOU.

"George Fistonich has been one of the most enterprising industry figures in spreading appreciation of wine ..."
NZ Herald

"Shortly after he made his announcement ... (of voluntary receivership) ... Mr Fistonich received a pile of awards from the Australian wine show in Canberra, including the most prestigious trophies ..."
Auckland Star

"Villa Maria Wines and its associated company Vidals, which went into receivership last week had consistantly produced superb wines, winning two gold medals last week, at the Australian National Wine Show in Canberra."
NZ Herald

"Wine distributors were united in their opinion that Villa Maria was "Steam rollered flat by the Brierly-Cooks-McWilliams combine."
National Business Review

"Villa Maria suffers Cruellest of Ironies"
Whangarei Advocate

"Neither the industry nor the consumer can afford to lose wine companies such as Villa and Vidals, which have constantly produced superb, quality wines ..."
Hospitality

We can't afford to lose these enterprises
Herald Tribune

"Manukau City's mayor Mr Barry Curtis has made the unusual step of asking his city's residents to support a business in need."
Manukau Courier

"We're part of the community – for 25 years we've sponsored bowling, cricket, tennis, rugby and rugby league clubs. We've helped cultural and community service clubs – and we need their support now."
George Fistonich Owner Villa Maria

"Villa Maria caused ... a sensation a few years ago by winning a gold medal for a flagon wine – bringing gold medal quality within the reach of the ordinary buyer."
NZ Herald

reflected in boosted sales of Villa Maria and Vidal Private Bin Wines – and overwhelming support from the media.

Last week 3 Auckland grape growers bought a full page in the Herald – thanking George for turning their grapes into award winning wines.

Last week, too, the entire staff of Villa Maria and Vidal chipped in and bought a half page in the Herald to demonstrate their loyalty to George Fistonich and his wineries.

Never before have so many New Zealanders pledged so much support for one small company.

And never before has that small company been so determined to fight back against the Goliaths of the wine industry and continue its remarkable tradition of producing wines that consistently win awards everywhere in the world.

VIDAL

VILLA MARIA
WINNING WINES

THIS SPREAD AND OVERLEAF

These three advertisements appeared in *The New Zealand Herald* as Villa Maria called on New Zealand wine buyers to show their support.

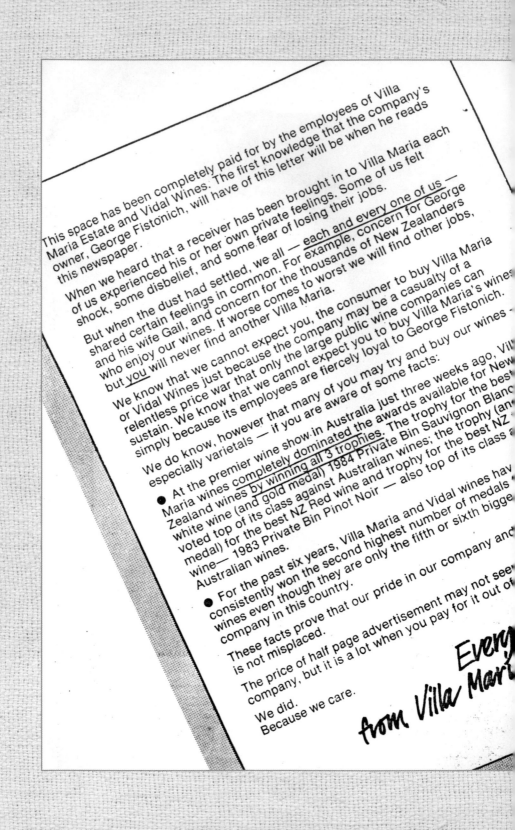

This space has been completely paid for by the employees of Villa Maria Estate and Vidal Wines. The first knowledge that the company's owner, George Fistonich, will have of this letter will be when he reads this newspaper.

When we heard that a receiver has been brought in to Villa Maria each of us experienced his or her own private feelings. Some of us felt shock, some disbelief, and some fear of losing their jobs.

But when the dust had settled, we all — each and every one of us — shared certain feelings in common. For example, concern for George and his wife Gail, and concern for the thousands of New Zealanders who enjoy our wines. If worse comes to worst we will find other jobs, but _you_ will never find another Villa Maria.

We know that we cannot expect you, the consumer to buy Villa Maria or Vidal Wines just because the company may be a casualty of a relentless price war that only the large public wine companies can sustain. We know that we cannot expect you to buy Villa Maria's wines simply because its employees are fiercely loyal to George Fistonich.

We do know, however that many of you may try and buy our wines — especially varietals — if you are aware of some facts:

● At the premier wine show in Australia just three weeks ago, Vill Maria wines completely dominated the awards available for New Zealand wines by winning all 3 trophies. The trophy for the best white wine (and gold medal) 1984 Private Bin Sauvignon Blanc voted top of its class against Australian wines; the trophy for the best NZ medal) for the best NZ Red wine and trophy for the best class a wine— 1983 Private Bin Pinot Noir — also top of its class Australian wines.

● For the past six years, Villa Maria and Vidal wines hav consistently won the second highest number of medals wines even though they are only the fifth or sixth bigge company in this country.

These facts prove that our pride in our company and is not misplaced.

The price of half page advertisement may not see company, but it is a lot when you pay for it out of

We did.
Because we care.

from Villa Mari *Every*

A Letter to Auckland Wine Drinkers From The Employees Of Villa Maria Estate And Vidal Wines.

ge
ries.

idal

to come to Auckland in time for a meeting on Sunday, 17 November.

Ahead of that meeting George called his office staff together, and on the evening of Friday, 15 November, he and Howell explained the situation to them. He took particular care in his explanation to his accounts clerk, Gay Connolly, because she was in the delicate situation of writing cheques and dealing with phone calls and demands from creditors. He also made sure Debbie Reid was one of the first to be told, because of her on-going relationship with Villa's contract growers.

Throughout the next day George called senior staff members into his office one at a time and told them what was happening. Then, on the Sunday, with all the out-of-towners duly in attendance, he called a meeting of all staff at the winery at 3pm. George had asked his daughter Karen to attend the meeting. She recalls her father's angst at having to explain the situation. 'Dad was trying to bolster their spirits and say, "Well, this is a challenge and don't look at receivership as the end of anything really — we're going to fight our way out of this situation." He told us then that this new guy Peter Howell was coming and would be helping him work through things. You do have this impression that receivers are like hatchet men and they're going to come in, look at the management and go: "Slice that out because it's not effective." But it quickly came evident that Howell realised that outside forces were putting us in an unsustainable position of selling at the lowest price just to keep cash flow. Peter gave an excellent speech and said that the receivership was not the fault of the staff and was just one of these things that happen.'

There was a strong sense of frustration at the news, but this was tempered somewhat by a passionate speech George gave in which he assured staff that with an energetic and positive response from the reps, Villa Maria could be saved.

The meeting then became a celebration — just as George had planned. 'After we had given them the news, instead of giving them a cup of tea we put the music on, ended up drinking vast quantities of wine, and had an amazing feed of crayfish and some champagne that had been donated. We turned it into a sort of pre-receivership party, a joyous occasion rather than doom and gloom. The combination of the decision to get all of the staff involved, to delay the receivership so that it coincided with the arrival home of the Australian awards, the positive attitude, and the good feeling that was generated by the staff party, was critical to how they supported the company during a very difficult time.' On the morning of Monday, 18 November, the day the receivership became public, George arranged to hold a press conference with Radio 1ZB, TVNZ and associated print media. It turned out to be a masterful public relations stratagem.

It was a very long day, yet despite the tension George retained his optimism. 'I went home that night to a house filled with family and supporters, like my sister Elsie and my cousin Tony Babich. They were all looking pretty mournful while I was on a real high. I suppose it was a bit of a relief to get over the first hurdle and talk to all the staff and see a positive response on the first day.'

In the days that followed, the 'Save Villa Maria' campaign was in full swing. The company received favourable publicity in the media, with the stories on radio and TV making it very clear that Villa Maria had been 'bulldozed' out of business. There were offers of support from wine retailers throughout the country, and broadcaster Leighton Smith even urged his listeners to go out and buy Villa Maria wines. Sales went up 35 per cent on the strength of the coverage; the reps were hyped-up.

In another bold move, on the day of the receivership George announced the launch of a new product: varietal casks. Although he had already committed to the rapid move from cask to bottled wine, he had stocks of high-quality wines — the result of Mark Polglase's treatment of a bumper 1985 harvest — which needed to be sold for cash-flow.

PRIOR TO THE RECEIVERSHIP, many observers in the wine industry as well as in business circles saw George as something of a survivor. But the seriousness of his financial plight could not be ignored. What happened over the next few weeks, however, turned a negative into a positive. Steve Bridges believes two events had a bigger impact than anyone might have predicted, and demonstrated that both Villa Maria's grape suppliers and its employees had a great degree of loyalty to, and even affection for, George as they worked hard to re-establish the company's credentials.

'First, three of George's Auckland contract grape growers, John Lambie, Ross Ellet and Ian Montgomerie, took out a full-page advertisement in *The New Zealand Herald* lamenting Villa Maria's fate and calling for the public's support. Second, George's staff also placed an advertisement in the *Herald* about a week or 10 days after the receivership was announced, saying what a great employer he was and what great wines he made,' Bridges remembers.

'I'll never forget calling Gail the day before the ad appeared, asking her to make sure George read the *Herald* at breakfast the next morning,' says Bridges. 'She subsequently told me that he got very emotional and was humbled by this demonstration of support by the people he employed.'

'I was bouyed by the positive attitude of all the staff,' says George. 'We were in war mode — ready to go and fight and sell our way out of receivership and to get back to business as usual.'

Villa Maria staff showed their commitment in other ways, too. They were being asked to work long hours, sometimes until 9pm, visiting customers, selling wine and drumming up support for Villa Maria. Many were being offered jobs by other wineries, yet during the six-month period of the receivership not one left the company or lost their job.

Karen Fistonich remembers the advertisements as 'a stroke of genius. They galvanised public and grower support for us, and I think also for the smaller industry players in general at the expense of the big guys. From then on we had no problem getting the cash flow in from the extra sales generated by the ads and by the publicity around the awards we got in Australia.'

In addition, the mayor of Manukau, Barry Curtis, called on the South Auckland community to support Villa Maria by purchasing its wines, in acknowledgement of the support George and his family had given the area's sports clubs and community organisations in the past. David Lange, Prime Minister at the time and local MP for Mangere, also made a point of commenting positively on the importance of Villa Maria to the South Auckland community. George also got support from former PM Rob Muldoon and from the new Leader of the Opposition, Jim McLay.

THE RELATIONSHIP WITH receiver Peter Howell was, on the whole, positive. Prior to discussion about the receivership the two men had not met, but Howell had had some involvement with the wine industry via an association with Vidal in the early 1970s. He therefore had a reasonable understanding of the state of the industry and the problems it was encountering.

As receiver, Howell's task was to sell Villa Maria and its assets and make sure the ANZ bank as a secured creditor got its money. 'George, understandably, was not happy about this, but he was left with no other choice,' remembers Howell. 'Receivership is never easy for any party, and I guess you always battle with people in a receivership situation. It's part of the process of two people who need and want different results.'

When Villa Maria was placed in receivership, a conversation took place between Peter Howell and Colin Herbert, CEO of liquor wholesaler Wilson Neill. Herbert, as one of Villa Maria's customers in Dunedin, was aware of the pressure George was under, and he suggested that George come down to Dunedin to discuss the situation, clearly with a view to Wilson Neill buying Villa Maria.

'I was feeling very positive and had already decided not to sell, and would retain my interest in the company,' says George. 'In the end I went to Dunedin anyway, to answer their questions about stock and things like that. I was under certain obligations to the receivers, so I did my duty, but with a strong degree of reluctance.'

Herbert was courteous, and the discussion amicable. 'He didn't make any formal offer, but was talking in the region of a million dollars, which considering the value of Villa Maria assets was very low.'

Years later, one-time would-be suitor Wilson Neill had its share of problems: in 2002 the company and six of its subsidiaries, with debts of more than $15 million, faced receivership.

GEORGE'S EFFORTS to save his business did not rely on public relations alone. He began a round of meetings with banks and potential investors, including Equiticorp. Until this time George's dealings with Equiticorp had been with company chairman Allan Hawkins, but deputy chairman Grant Adams was close to the situation, managing the debt on behalf of Equiticorp, and it was during a discussion with Adams about his financial problems that Adams made George an offer. George had told Adams that he had been speaking to Wilson Neill, and that they were talking a very low offer. Adams then told George that he was quite passionate about wine and was prepared to make a personal investment (rather than an extension of the loan from Equiticorp): he would buy half of Villa Maria if George could find someone to buy the other half. George immediately saw the potential in this offer. 'I was determined to get back in control of the company, so I did some sums and figured that, if we sold our house in Remuera and mortgaged everything else we had, I would come close to raising enough money to buy half the company back.'

The two men took the proposal to Peter Howell, who remembers the meeting well. 'Very soon after receivership, George introduced an investor, Grant Adams, who was willing to purchase a share of the business, allowing the ANZ to be paid out and enabling the receivership to be terminated. But that left a backlog of creditors, largely grape growers, and the unanswered question of how they could be paid out. There were strong indications from George that Villa Maria Wines could continue to trade. He had wine and he had access to grapes, but a company in receivership cannot trade. So, in what was a somewhat unusual move, we formed a new company, Villa Maria Estate Ltd. This avoided having a company trading in receivership, and gave George a chance to pay off the old company's creditors, because if Villa Maria Wines' other creditors, who were largely grape growers, didn't get paid off, the future of any new company would be very difficult.'

Out of the fire of receivership
a strong commercial bond
emerged: Coopers & Lybrand
receiver Peter Howell with
George Fistonich.

Villa Maria Estate Ltd was set up with three shareholders, each of whom had a one-third share. Grant Adams owned a share, George owned a share, and, in an arrangement with creditors of Villa Maria Wines, Peter Howell took a third share on their behalf, in effect becoming a creditors' representative. A scheme was agreed that would see remaining creditors being paid out over a period of four years.

The winding-up of Villa Maria Wines wiped out the equity George had in the company he had established. In order to purchase his third share of Villa Maria Estate, he sold the family home in Remuera where they had lived since 1981, and mortgaged the land he had bought in Clevedon as a 21-year-old to borrow $800,000.

Then, in another unusual move, Grant Adams induced the BNZ bank to lend the new company, Villa Maria Estate, enough funds to pay out the remaining creditors in total, thus sparing the company and its shareholders the long period of having to drip-feed creditors what they were owed. On this basis, and with the consent of the ANZ, the receiver was withdrawn, and the new company, Villa Maria Estate Ltd, became the trading entity at the end of April 1986.

That year Villa Maria won its first major international award — the trophy for Best Gewürztraminer in the World at the International Wine and Spirits competition in London — the first of the many international awards the company and George would go on to win over the next 25 years. George and Gail travelled to London to collect the award at the House of Commons. The same year the Villa Maria Reserve Chardonnay won the Air New Zealand Trophy.

BY THE END of 1986 Villa Maria was once again trading profitably, having achieved what George describes as 'a miraculous recovery'.

'We had initially entered into a four-year scheme of arrangement with the creditors, but with a combination of Grant Adams's equity, and some support from the BNZ, we paid everything off within a year. Under receivership you don't pay any interest on the long-term debt, so I basically gave away the opportunity to have the benefit of an interest-free loan for four years. The judge who discharged the receivership congratulated me on that, and said that it was very rare for somebody to do that.'

George's success in staving off long-term receivership was recognised in other ways. In November 1986 he and Peter Howell were asked to make a presentation to the Institute for International Research at a conference in Wellington.

At the conference George was introduced by Sir Kenneth Cork, GBE, DLitt, FCA, who painted a glowing picture of the efforts Villa Maria had made to protect its interests. Karen recalls her father's delight at being given the opportunity to tell his story. 'About the time of the receivership I went to work at ANZ head office in Wellington. A year later, while I was still down there, Dad called me and told me he had to come to Wellington with Peter Howell to talk to a conference for receivers in Wellington. They were talking about Villa Maria as a case study of a receivership that had been managed with a positive outcome. That to me was incredible, because it was such an amazing turnaround. He had gone into receivership, which was all very stressful, not knowing what the outcome is going to be, and only a year later he was there in Wellington presenting this successful case study — a receivership where they identified the management as not at fault.'

The tension of the receivership took its toll on George, but Karen believes it taught her father a lot, too. 'At the very least it taught him to stay healthy. Dad wasn't a very healthy person in his late forties. He smoked heavily, was overweight, didn't exercise, and worked very long hours. At his seventieth birthday, a friend, Maurice Langdon, actually piped up and said: "I met George in his forties, and I didn't think he would make 50, let alone 70." We were a bit taken aback, the way he said it. But we knew what he meant. I told Dad, "I know exactly what Maurice means." Dad's father was 62 when he died, his older brother was 59, and his younger brother Peter passed away when he was 54. Dad's now totally self-righteous about being healthy and believes we all should follow his example.'

As George now chuckles, 'I ended up losing half the company, but I managed to buy it back. It had some benefits. I lost two stone in weight and began an exercise regime that I keep to this day!'

13
STABILITY
RETURNS

In the months after the receivership ended, Villa Maria Estate was performing well. Peter Howell was invited by George to stay on as an advisor to the company once the creditors had been paid out. Howell was privy to the issues being dealt with at board level, and believed strongly that the company would survive and could trade profitably. He thought Villa Maria had been through a bad patch and he saw brighter days ahead; the industry was picking up.

Esk Valley winemaker Gordon
Russell hand-plunging in
the concrete vats originally
built by the Bird family for
Glenvale and which are still
used for the Esk Valley reds.

'It seemed entirely logical for me to engage Peter's services,' says George. 'Peter was a great support to me during this period, and with his counsel I learned a great deal about financial structures, and I grew to respect his sage advice enormously. He is a complete gentleman, one of the most direct and matter-of-fact people I have ever met, but utterly honest and well-intentioned.'

In 1986, production at Villa Maria was once again accelerating. The change in emphasis from cask to bottled wine was proving highly successful, and the company's demand for high-quality grapes was continuing to grow. The subject of grape supply was a frequent agenda item at board level, and around this time a decision was made to explore the option of buying further contracts in Hawke's Bay.

The first option they explored was Glenvale Winery and Cellars, established in 1933 by Robert Bird, and one of the early Hawke's Bay wineries that had a good reputation for making port and sherry. When Bird retired, his son Bob Bird Jnr took over, and later his sons, Don and Robbie — young men in their mid to late twenties — took charge.

They had started to produce very small quantities of varietal wine under the Esk Valley brand, but were not really geared up for producing table wines. George had had a fair bit to do with Glenvale in the previous three or four years, and was privy to the financial strain the company was under. He also knew they had access to a cache of growers in the region.

'When the price war began, the Bird boys had rung me a few times to see what was happening with other family-owned companies and to get some sort of idea on what could be done about the pricing issues. They seemed good people and I gave them as much help as I could, but I was under my own kind of pressure and could not involve myself too much. I went into receivership, but as a third-generation company they still had quite a bit of capital and were able to weather the storm for longer. But, as a direct result of the price war, they were also starting to go downhill and beginning to lose their equity.'

Support for the purchase came immediately from Peter Howell, who had, by coincidence, been appointed an unofficial advisor to Esk Valley Wines at the same time he was advising the board of Villa Maria Estate. 'Glenvale had good assets, but I thought the main thing was that they used to sell grape juice without alcohol. They had quite a big business, and I thought that would add to George's business.

Convinced that it was a good idea to buy Glenvale, with its highly productive vineyards for growing varietal grapes, plus extensive storage facilities on a stunning site, George put a proposal to the BNZ bank. With the support of Grant Adams's strong financial status and the strong encouragement of George's BNZ manager, Alan Milne, Villa Maria was also able to add 30,000 square feet of extra production and warehouse facilities to the winery in Kirkbride Road.

'Alan's positive attitude was a breath of fresh air. He believed that with adequate funding we would be very successful, and so worked with us to gain the capital we needed. Unfortunately he was later to become a victim of the sharemarket crash, which forced many banks into blaming the lending policies of its managers for their troubles,' remembers Howell.

'We had earned a few Brownie points by discharging our receivership much earlier than expected, and were also able to point to growing sales and huge public and trade support for our wine,' says George of the relationship with the BNZ. 'Grant Adams was also riding high at the time and was reputed to be worth about $100 million, and so the bank looked favourably on the deal and lent us the money we needed.'

George paid around $1 million for Glenvale. Howell says the price was sufficient for the owners to have an equity and to pay their creditors. 'They didn't get as much as they would have liked, but they couldn't carry on anyway.'

The Bird brothers, appreciative of the assistance George had given them along the way, welcomed the deal. Initially they both stayed on, but when they resigned George put in Tony Hooper, Villa Maria's assistant winemaker, for a couple of years. He also immediately eliminated the Glenvale brand, and accelerated the conversion of the company from a reasonably large fortified wine producer into a boutique winery under the Esk Valley brand. When Grant Edmonds was later appointed winemaker, he made sure the place operated independently but under the Villa Maria winemaking philosophy, and it began to tick over very nicely.

At the time of the purchase by Villa Maria, Glenvale had been making around 50 different products, including a collection of liqueurs and cocktail mixes. There was one product, however, that nobody had counted on. Some time later a Glenvale sparkling grape juice was bottled at Villa and released into the trade. Subsequently the Villa Maria team began to hear stories of bottles blowing up. Apparently the juice had not been sulphured properly, and after a while any little movement caused the bottle to explode. When George found out that someone at the winery had tried to conceal their error he hit the roof. An immediate recall was organised and the problem rectified.

BUT THE GOOD times were to be short-lived. In October 1987 the sharemarket crashed, and Equiticorp, to whom Grant Adams was so closely linked, was one of the first of the previously adored market high-flyers who would shortly thereafter plunge to earth. When Equiticorp spectacularly failed, Grant Adams's wealth was more or less wiped out. It's not hard to see how the BNZ, which had not only lent Equiticorp money but had also been persuaded by Adams to lend money to Villa Maria, would now have lost confidence in Equiticorp and, by association, in Adams. Once again, a bank, was threatening to wind up Villa Maria.

Meetings between George and his bankers were frequent, but one was more memorable than others. George had been asked to the BNZ to discuss the issue of refinancing. He took along Steve Bridges. As Bridges recalls it: 'The bankers were impassive throughout our meeting, which exasperated both of us. George finally erupted, telling them in no uncertain terms that they had no heart and no interest in his business — that, among other things, they had never even come out once to see his winery and operation. He was highly emotional. In all the years I've worked with George, I have only seen him angry that once.'

George also remembers the occasion. 'We were taken into the naughty boys' room and I felt as though I was being blamed for the Equiticorp downfall. So I got bloody angry and told them exactly what I felt.'

Others, too, remember that meeting. Many years later the BNZ manager at the time approached George at an event they were both attending. 'He asked if I remembered him. I said no, and he said, "Well, I will never forget you telling us all exactly what you thought of us. But I have watched your progress over the years and really admire your success. Congratulations." '

Even so, George knew he would have to change the shareholding to save the company; Adams would be the victim. 'George felt exposed by the fact that Grant Adams had evidently fallen out of favour with the bank and had for George become a public relations liability,' remembers Peter Howell. Eventually Adams agreed to sell out to long-time Villa Maria grape grower Ian Montgomerie, who put up $1 million to buy Adams's 50 per cent share. George agreed to pay interest to Montgomerie, and arranged to buy back at least 40 per cent from him within 12 months. This would give him 90 per cent ownership of Villa. Peter Howell describes this as a 'clean deal'.

Avon Carpenter got straight to work seeking the capital George would need to make this arrangement work. Even so, they were not yet on home base. In spite of the restructuring plan, a new BNZ team assessed the debt-to-equity ratios, decided Villa Maria was an extreme case, and put the business into its recovery unit. The BNZ got very close to appointing a receiver, but Howell and George managed to talk them out of it.

A year later things had once again settled. George had purchased back the 40 per cent as agreed, and Ian Montgomerie with his 10 per cent became a shareholder and continued on the Villa Maria board as chairman. 'Ian was a very old and valued friend, and he did a very good job when he was on the board. He had a good understanding of what grape growing is all about and what makes a successful relationship between grower and wine maker,' says George. 'I valued his involvement.'

THE OCTOBER 1987 sharemarket crash threw George yet another curve ball, but he shielded his winemakers from the worst aspects of the fallout and made sure the team had everything it needed. Just as he had during the receivership, 'he was once again engrossed in sorting that all out, and he left us to do our own thing and really showed a huge amount of trust in us and our ability,' says Kym Milne.

In 1988 came another king hit. The economy had begun to settle and business was once more really beginning to hum when a massive storm known as Cyclone Bola hit New Zealand, causing huge damage in Hawke's Bay and Gisborne. Again, Villa was plunged into a situation where it was short of the grapes it was most after: Chardonnay, Sauvignon Blanc and Gewürztraminer.

Even so, there was plenty of good news amidst the struggle. It was a period when some great wines were being produced, including some outstanding Chardonnay and Sauvignon Blanc from Gisborne grapes. Despite the backroom troubles, in the public realm Villa Maria's reputation was once again growing rapidly, helped tremend-ously by its continuing success in wine competitions; the fact that the market was now fully aware of how good Villa wine was stood it in good stead. In 1989, the 1987 Reserve Cabernet Sauvignon Merlot won Best Red and Top Wine of the Show at the Sydney Top 100 Wine Awards, much to the consternation of the Australians.

Steve Smith had travelled the wine regions, organising contracts

Jeremy and Judy Waldron, shown
here working with their brand-new
Rapaura Road plantings, were the
first Marlborough grape growers
to sign a contract with Villa Maria.
They still supply Villa Maria today.

with new growers and persuading existing growers to replant with the classic varieties George wanted: Sauvignon Blanc, Chardonnay, Riesling and Gewürztraminer. And in 1989 wine exports to the United Kingdom began to take off. Twice a year Kym Milne would travel there and tour around Hatch Mansfield's outlets, doing tastings and promoting Villa wines.

Steve Smith was relishing his role at Villa Maria. George had hired him in 1987 when Villa Maria was still in a delicate financial situation. He'd had another very good offer, from Cloudy Bay, whose Marlborough Sauvignon Blanc was beginning to turn heads, but there was something about the offer from George that made Smith decide to accept it. 'If you'd looked at it rationally, it looked like a crazy thing to do. George was not long out of his financial trouble, and some of the vineyards needed more money invested in them but money was short. But he told me about his plans to turn the whole company around, and how he wanted people who wanted to be part of that. That just really appealed to me. It was a chance for me to stamp my mark professionally. Plus, when George really wants something he's pretty persuasive.'

Even so, Smith chopped and changed his mind, phoning the Villa Maria receptionist three times to ask her to tell George that he wouldn't be taking the job. 'Luckily George doesn't normally get to his messages until the end of the day, so he didn't get the last one in which I'd said no!' Smith laughs.

Once he began work, everything that George had indicated would be possible was in fact possible. 'George gives you just enough rope to hang yourself,' says Smith. 'He let me do so much in the vineyard, but he also let me have some input into the blends and into the marketing and PR side of the business. I was allowed to get involved in so much and I learnt so much.'

He came to appreciate just how determined George was on continuing to improve quality, and how George had an instinctive feel for wine. 'The thing about George is that, of all the heads of the large wine operations in New Zealand, he is a genuine wine person. He loves every part of the industry, but especially what goes into the bottles.'

Smith would leave Villa Maria for Craggy Range in 1998. One of an impressive roll-call of Villa 'graduates' who have gone on to stellar careers with other winemakers or to do their own thing, he looks back on his time at the company with fondness. And he has some amusing Villa Maria stories to tell, stories he tells with the aplomb and humour typical of the larger-than-life characters who people the New Zealand wine industry.

'George loves it when people tell him he can't do something,' he says. 'I remember the first time we bought grapes from Chris Pask in Hawke's Bay in 1987. Chris had been saying that he wouldn't sell his grapes to George Fistonich, because he felt the receivership had hurt grape growers. Well, what people forget is that George has a great capacity for staying up very late, drinking wine and smoking cigars. That might not be so obvious these days when he's the picture of health. In 1987 George had eventually managed to get Chris to sell him some grapes. And in 1988 Chris was saying again that he wouldn't sell, but after a very long session at Vidal's one night, George emerged with a contract written on the back of a cigarette packet!'

Having signed its first grape-grower contract with Jeremy and Judy Waldron in 1988, 1990 was the first year that Villa Maria started taking significant quantities of grapes out of Marlborough, picking the fruit cold and transporting the grapes to the Auckland winery by road. George could see that Marlborough was going to boom, and knew he would have to find another approach. At the huge 1991 vintage Villa Maria picked even more out of Marlborough, but this time used a contract winemaking facility in the province, where the wine was made under Milne's direction.

That year George got himself into a major spat with the New Zealand Wine Institute. Villa Maria was taking a lot of Sauvignon Blanc out of Marlborough, but the company still had contracts with Gisborne growers for Sauvignon and had an oversupply. Marlborough had become the preferred region for Sauvignon Blanc, and Gisborne Savignon Blanc was now almost impossible to sell in a bottle. So George arranged to export it to the United Kingdom in the form of bulk wine, to be distributed there through Grants of St James, and sold under the Stowells of Chelsea brand as New Zealand Sauvignon Blanc. In doing so he unintentionally became the first wine producer to export bulk New Zealand wine to the United Kingdom. Other producers were not happy, arguing that cask wine (as this bulk wine would end up being) undermined the quality brand that New Zealand was trying to promote. They voiced their disapproval to the Wine Institute.

George, who was a key member of the guild, was summoned to a meeting where his competitors could vent their frustration. Instead, to make the case more independently, he elected to send Milne along to put the Villa Maria case. 'He spent a few hours schooling me up on the details and what I was going to say,' remembers Milne. 'His argument was that the wine was going into outlets that had not yet been exposed to New Zealand wine, and that it was in fact beneficial for the New Zealand brand to have new people being exposed to New Zealand wine. He also wanted me to point out that when taxes were included, producing a three-litre cask of New Zealand Sauvignon Blanc was about the same price as a 750ml bottle, so no one could claim it was cheap and nasty. In fact, the wine we were sending was very good and not just crap that was bottled and labelled. Anyway I went into the meeting to find that the representative of the New Zealand Wine Institute based in London was there, and she actually spoke in favour of the wine and what we were doing,' he says.

In spite of some rumblings, the small tiff fizzled out. Once Villa Maria had exhausted its supply of Gisborne Sauvignon, it stopped sending bulk wine to the United Kingdom — even though, as George notes, later other institute members found ways to do exactly the same thing.

BY THIS TIME George's winemaker Kym Milne was 30, had completed his Master of Wine qualification, was recently married, and was thinking about moving on to Pacific Wines in the United Kingdom. 'I had originally come to Villa with a view to staying for a couple of vintages, but when George made me head winemaker I knew I would be mad not to make the most of the opportunity. I had a plan that I

George with winemaker
Kym Milne.

would spend five years travelling the wine world, doing vintages here and there and learning as much as I could before heading back to Australia. Of course things didn't go quite according to plan.'

When did he make the decision to go, he had no regrets. 'I discussed things with George, who was, as always, really supportive, and we talked about how there was a good team in place so the move was not going to leave him in the lurch. I gave him six to seven months' notice and said I would wait until after vintage before leaving.'

Milne knew he was leaving Villa with a very capable and skilled team. 'Grant Edmonds had sorted out Esk, and Kate Radburnd had done great things at Vidal's.' But a smooth handover was not to be. George felt that the wine quality had dropped and decided to take drastic action. 'Two weeks before vintage I ended up changing the whole team.' He then called Michelle Richardson, who had been at Villa Maria for a few months in 1992 as a temporary cellar hand, and asked whether she would be senior assistant to his newly appointed winemaker, Grant Edmonds. During her earlier stint with the company George had watched Richardson at work, and had been impressed. Milne had also thought 'she'd showed some pretty good skills over vintage, and I could see she was destined for success as a winemaker'. It was to be another of George's inspired hires.

George has always rated Kym Milne as one of the greats, and has continued to seek his advice. 'Not only was he very successful as a winemaker, and also as a businessman and blender, but another of his great skills was as a trainer,' he says of Milne. 'He trained Grant Edmonds, and guided both Elise Montgomery, Kate Radburnd and Michelle Richardson as well as a host of others while he was here. He is like me in some ways — a bit of a micro-manager. When he was here, he would just call me and let me know what was going on.'

Since 1992 Milne has travelled back to New Zealand once, sometimes twice, a year, to lend a hand when the blends are decided. In more recent times Milne's busy schedule has meant he has not been able to return in person, but George continues to stay in contact, 'calling to discuss wine with me when he feels another perspective is required'.

235

RIGHT

George tasting wines
for final blending.

BELOW

Steve Smith, Michelle
Richardson, Grant
Edmonds and George
pose with another
trophy haul at an
Air New Zealand
Wine Awards dinner.

MICHELLE RICHARDSON, who now has her own label, would go on to make stellar wines at Villa Maria. She describes her relationship with George as 'rather tumultuous, built on respect, loyalty and a fair whack of frustration — on my part and no doubt on his. He offered me the job without any interview, based on a brief 10-minute meeting we had had about nine months earlier and a conversation which at the time confused me. I now know that George was analysing me, as he does so often with people, and acquiring a gut feeling about me. This shows a side of George I saw consistently throughout my time there: his reliance on gut feeling, and his ability to ride through any stressful situation. He remains relatively calm, clear-headed and pragmatic. He is not averse to taking risks, and it was a risk to hire me.'

Richardson, like so many others, speaks of George's propensity to make entirely intuitive decisions about the character of the people he employs. 'If the first impression does not go well, there is little anyone can do to make up for it. Once George believes he has the measure of someone, there is nothing that you can do to change that, and deep down people knew it. I saw several examples of people vying for his approval, but never quite getting it. It caused them to dislike him but revere him at the same time. They eventually left, yet I think if George offered them his trust now, they would jump at the chance and all would be forgiven.'

But Richardson is adamant that George's ways of dealing with people does not necessarily lead to the stifling of opportunity to develop both professionally and personally. 'If George trusts you, he leaves you alone; if he is not sure of your work, he'll watch you and involve himself to the nth degree. It drives people mad, but it never ceased to surprise me how they would never say anything to him. This style, rather than teaching the person something, often stifled them to the point where they showed little initiative, often infuriating George more. He is an avid people-watcher, and I always get the feeling he is laying down more information with every word you utter, filing it away in that labyrinth brain of his. I think if he did not go down the path of winemaking, he could have been a psychiatrist — or perhaps a charismatic religious cult leader.'

The friction between George and Richardson sometimes boiled over. 'George respects people who respect him but tell it like it is. I think that is why we got on — or didn't at times. I have had some huge verbal fights with George. Shouting, slamming of doors. While it shows my lack of emotional maturity at the time, George's completely unfazed attitude also showed a side that perhaps enjoyed it. It gave him an outlet to shout, too, and of course feel in control.'

During her 10 years at Villa Maria, Richardson says she had her psyche probed various times. 'The first test was done without my knowledge. I wanted to be insulted, but I was actually intrigued and liked the unorthodox approach. And those results were scarily accurate. I began to think that there were more interesting sides to this new boss of mine, and throughout the years we had many interesting discussions on anything but wine.'

While she found George's continual delving into her psyche frustrating and annoying, Richardson admits the results contributed positively to her development. 'His unorthodox approach wove in and out of favour. One year we were paid to attend Transcendental Meditation classes, as George had found TM very helpful. If he enjoyed a book (always non-fiction) he would buy 50 copies and distribute them amongst his managers and staff. That is how I got to read *Sun Tzu — The Art of War for Executives* by Donald G Krause, which was at times an apt book to have on hand. I also think that everything George does is with a fair amount of calculation, often leaving people behind trying to sort out where he is going with something.'

Richardson hesitates to pigeon-hole her former employer. 'He has many sides, and the type of person you are or the relationship you have with him will determine what sides you see. During my time at Villa Maria I saw a man who was at times a bully, frustrating, distant, infuriating, interesting, inspiring, generous, cheeky, fun-to-be-with and not-so-fun-to-be-with. Basically, he's a pretty interesting human being, and one who inspires a bewildering degree of loyalty from many of his staff.'

14
EXPANSION

Inaugural Prese...
...994
...Awarded to...
Esk Valle...
Reserve Me...lot M...

In July 1986 Montana Wines took over Penfolds, thus becoming the largest producer in the country, with around 40 per cent of the market. The two operations were merged on the one site in Glen Innes, Auckland. This was to be winemaking on a massive scale; the company was well on its way to becoming a major corporate player.

Gail and George at a wine awards
dinner, with Villa Maria's trophies
proudly displayed.

Villa Maria's Kirkbride Road winery looked tiny by comparison. But Villa Maria was not quaking in its boots. Instead the company was working towards growth via export. The first major breakthrough came on 10 May 1988, when the Grants of St James subsidiary Hatch Mansfield placed a major order. This was subsequently increased on 7 June 1988, and on 22 July a total of 1265 cases — 250 cases of Villa Maria Reserve Chardonnay 1987 and Reserve Cabernet Sauvignon 1986, and 1015 cases of Private Bin Sauvignon Blanc 1987 and Cabernet Sauvignon 1987 — were put on board the ship *Ivangrad* and shipped off to the United Kingdom.

The next shipment was in early March 1989, and this was followed by another in early May of the same year. 'After that we would send an order out every couple of months, whereas now it's about every day,' laughs Ian Clark.

The innovation that typified Villa Maria's marketing efforts in those days was well illustrated by the approach taken to promote the brand in the United Kingdom. In the absence of money to spend on above-the-line advertising in Britain, it was decided to print a single sheet that listed all the Villa Maria wines available in the United Kingdom, along with a return fax form. This was then inserted into 7000 copies of the November edition of *Cuisine* magazine. The idea was that local readers of what was New Zealand's pre-eminent wine and food publication would then take the opportunity to purchase wine as a Christmas gift for their relatives and friends in the United Kingdom.

'*Cuisine* readers would return the order form to us in Auckland and we would fax it to Hatch Mansfield, who would arrange delivery of the wine to consumers in the United Kingdom in time for Christmas. We sold a lot of wine that way, and increased our exposure hugely,' says Clark. 'For example, we may have received 2000 orders from New Zealand-based customers, but their English relatives would share the wine with their friends over Christmas; they would like the wine, and in turn would seek it out from local suppliers. We made no money out of it, but we did it for every November for about five years, and it was a very successful way of getting people to try our wine and establish our brand in the UK, and so it worked really well on a cost-recovery basis.' The United Kingdom quickly became Villa Maria's biggest market by volume, continuing to expand year on year.

IN 1986 a Canadian, Paul Corley, contacted George. Corley had worked creating advertising for a number of international brands, including Rolls-Royce, and for various airlines around the world, and had arrived in New Zealand looking for work. He came with a recommendation from New Zealand's own advertising guru David Innes, who didn't know Corley personally but was aware of his work through a mutual acquaintance. George put Corley on a contract and set him to work on a complete overhaul of the company's labels, letterheads, logos and envelopes, including all the stationery and branding for Vidal and Esk Valley.

Corley was to remain on contract to Villa for a year. Steve Bridges briefed Corley and wrote the personality statements for each of the brands, and Corley worked under the management of David Innes, mostly out of Innes's Auckland office. Innes and Bridges credit Corley with some outstanding work, especially on the Villa Maria and Esk Valley brands. It became one of the most comprehensive packaging renewal projects in New Zealand brand history. Such was its complexity that Bridges recalls that a five-minute video, hosted by prominent radio broadcaster Leighton Smith, was commissioned to assist in explaining

Pickers on the
prized Esk
Valley Terraces
in Hawke's Bay.

the changes and the reasons behind them. It was taken to trade functions throughout the country to launch the new look.

Innes remembers Corley as difficult to manage, 'in some ways quite mad — like many advertising creatives'. Innes takes some of the credit for Corley's Esk Valley label design. 'Corley came to me frustrated because he couldn't get a shot of both the terraced vineyards at Esk and the church which was on the other side of the road. I suggested he move the church.'

Corley's Esk Valley labels were used from 1989 until 2010, and his Villa Maria labels have been kept fairly much intact ever since.

IN 1989 GEORGE expanded Esk's harvest potential by establishing The Terraces Vineyard on the steep slopes behind the winery, a project he paid for by cutting down a stand of pine trees that stood on the property. He planted the site with the very first Malbec grapes in the Hawke's Bay, thereby creating yet another milestone. In 1991 Grant Edmonds produced the first wine from The Terraces fruit, and since that time it has gone on to become one of New Zealand's iconic wines.

Later, in 1999, George pioneered another variety in the Hawke's Bay when he planted the first Verdelho grapes in New Zealand, in the Esk vineyard in Gimblett Gravels. 'Esk has been very good for us,' he says. 'It's a great brand with some excellent wine. Grant made some really good red wines there, which in some ways were a bit eccentric, a bit like Grant really. He's a hell of a nice guy. He's very organised and a systems person, with a very dry and unusual sense of humour. He worked with Michelle Richardson as her assistant for three years. They're great friends, but some of their verbal exchanges were unprintable. They made great reading!

'Gordon Russell [the current Esk winemaker] is similar in some ways. Gordon is an amazing winemaker and often quite courageous. I have a hell of a lot of time for Gordon. He's really loyal and extremely passionate, and is capable of producing outstanding red wines. I think he's a real asset and is in just the right place at Esk.'

Esk Valley continues to add to the Villa Maria Estate medal haul.

Gordon Russell at work
at Esk Valley.

The 1992, 1994, 1995, 1999 and 2000 vintages of the Esk Valley Reserve Red were the top wines in *Cuisine* magazine's annual review, and all other vintages have been in the Top 10 of the magazine's annual list.

It is not only the Esk reds that have gained it prominence. In 2000 the company pioneered the making of low-alcohol German-style Riesling in the Hawke's Bay, and at the 2001 *Winestate* magazine awards in Australia the Esk Valley 1999 Reserve Chardonnay won the Chardonnay Trophy. In 2004 at the Sydney International Wine Competition, the Esk Valley 2003 Reserve Chardonnay took the Trophy for Best Chardonnay.

Esk Valley winemaker
Gordon Russell.

15
THE BOSS

If George's management style in the mid-1980s was all about picking the right people, then the gregarious Angela Lewis, who fits snugly into the group of George's 'chosen', is typical. Villa Maria's corporate relationships manager since 2011, Lewis first came to Villa Maria in 1984 as a sales representative, joining a staff of 30, around half of whom were also in sales.

Long-time Villa employee
Angela Lewis.

Lewis's territory stretched from Northland to throughout Auckland, where she was responsible for having Villa Maria wines listed in as many wine shops, liquor outlets, hotels, restaurants and bars as possible.

Lewis had been a teacher and had no serious sales experience when George offered her the job, but she had the chutzpah George loves to see. In 1987, soon after Villa Maria came out of receivership, George promoted her to acting sales manager. It was a major career opportunity — and challenge — he had thrown her. She jumped at it. 'The energy around the place was infectious, and we all worked long hours during and especially after the receivership, when the support from the community was tremendous and our reputation just grew and grew. Our biggest customers — Wineworths, Wilson Neill and the Jakicevich brothers (owners of the Auckland wine stores, Glengarrys) — were absolutely amazing and stocked large quantities of our bottle wines. We also received great support from all the independent and privately owned wine shops, Robbie Burns, and New Zealand Wines and Spirits and their liquor retail chains, then owned by Lion Breweries.

'George insisted we look after them really well, and they returned the favour by really promoting our wine. In one store, I think it was Wineworths, a customer walked in and said: "I want a bottle of wine from that guy who is in financial trouble"! The other liquor channels, owned by Brierley's, offered very little support.'

Lewis recalls many other high-profile supporters, including restaurateurs Tony Adcock (of Harbourside), Judith Tabron (then running Ramses Bar and Grill) and the Tony's Steak House group amongst others, who took a proactive role in promoting Villa Maria, sometimes removing from their wine lists the wines from competitors Cooks and McWilliam's.

In 1989 Lewis became group sales manager, working with an ever-expanding team promoting wines from Villa, Vidal and the more recently acquired Esk Valley. The rapidly changing market demanded equally rapid responses, the enthusiastic and energetic marketing strategy was sometimes unco-ordinated, and George had a propensity to be personally involved in most decisions, which left some feeling as though there was little opportunity for professional growth. Lewis feels that George is, in fact, more open to personal growth than many other employers. 'George puts a phenomenal level of investment into training, and not just in-house training. If he thinks there is benefit in staff doing a personal development course, he will not hesitate in making that happen. In the early days we would have four to five conferences a year, and he provided great support by allowing me to engage the very best sales trainers I could find. We used those occasions to ensure the team had all the skills required, and, because George has a "New Age" side, sometimes the training would include unconventional techniques such as NLP (Neurolinguistic Programming), visualisation and meditation, which he felt could be used to overcome stress. We always had a great time at these conferences, making sure we were keeping the team motivated. George would join in and knew each team member personally. Many of these people are friends today, and we love to reminisce about the old days and the hilarious times we had together.'

In 1991, when the law was altered to permit wine sales in super-markets, Lewis assumed responsibility for managing Villa Maria's supermarket accounts. She left Villa in 1996 to have a son, but returned on a part-time basis less than a year later in a trade marketing role.

Meanwhile, George employed Sue Clark as sales and marketing manager, replacing himself in the position. Clark was a straight-shooter, and while not all staff initially warmed to her high-octane style Lewis felt she joined at just the right time. 'She brought in an entirely new perspective and added a level of professionalism and a knowledge of how supermarkets worked that we hadn't had. She arranged for us to have market-share figures, and we had charts that told us how much we were selling and volumes, etc. It was something I could not have done; I simply did not have the experience.'

It was around this time that Lewis also took responsibility for managing Villa's role in festivals and events, a task which was to become increasingly broad and complex over the next few years. Yet another change occurred in 2005, when George asked Lewis to take charge of on-premise sales. In addition, Lewis has retained responsibility for sponsorship and promotional activity. In 2011 she took responsibility for the expanding area of corporate relations. It's a role she relishes.

Lewis remembers George's distinctive interview style. 'He would ask really personal questions, questions you wouldn't able to ask nowadays, like "Do you have a boyfriend?"' She is adamant that this wasn't prying. 'George has only ever been completely above-board in all things, but it was him trusting his intuition. Before making a decision he needs to form a deeper impression of the person he is interviewing, and he was never satisfied with just knowing your employment history.'

SHE SAYS GEORGE cares deeply about the welfare of his staff, both in a personal and a professional sense. 'In all the years I have worked for George and in all the circumstances I have seen him, including some very rowdy staff functions, I have never ever seen him be over-familiar. In fact, I know he is very uncomfortable when he sees anyone behaving in a way he believes inappropriate. In every conversation he is a gentleman, and unless he is enquiring about your wellbeing or your family he only ever talks about wine and business. He will ask some of us our impressions about others in the company, how they are doing and what their reactions might be given a set of circumstances, but you know it's because he cares or is concerned and just wants information that will help him manage a situation better.'

Lewis says he also deserves respect for the way women are treated at Villa Maria. 'Right from the very early days, George has taken and promoted staff on merit, and sees women as entirely capable of doing the same tasks as men. He is way ahead of his time in that.'

Another to recognise George's commitment to personal development is national business development manager Sue Bird. Bird joined Villa Maria in 1987 and has held a number of senior roles in the sales force since that time. 'I've never contemplated leaving Villa,' she says. 'If ever I have felt remotely restless, I simply talk to George and next thing my job changes and I get new challenges and new responsibilities to reinvigorate me. He is amazing like that. He has this uncanny ability to find ways of keeping things interesting, and if that means arranging extra training or putting us on a course or whatever he makes it happen. I think it's because George, while always being the boss and the decision-maker, likes to be really close to the action. At sales conferences George would always be the first to arrive and the last to leave. Often late at night we would be in someone's room having a few drinks and George would be with rest of us, lying across the beds talking and planning.

'His totally hands-on approach can be frustrating because sometimes you feel you can't make a move without involving him — about even in the smallest matters — but the upside is knowing that there is a totally consistent approach in this company and everyone knows where they stand.'

Bird's loyalty to her boss is uncompromising 'At Villa you are part of the family, and as with any family you are encouraged to talk to others, to make your feelings known and to offer opinions. You always know that George will take the final decision, but I know he listens because there have been occasions when years after we have discussed something he will raise it again as if to say, "I remember what you said". I can't imagine any other company where staff are

Vidal winemaker
Elise Montgomery and
George with a clutch
of trophies.

treated with such concern and, when trusted by the head of the company, can be so intimately involved.

'A case in point is when George first purchased the site of the new winery in Montgomerie Road. On a Friday he would load a bunch of us into the four-wheel-drive and bring us up as far as the entrance, and we would all pile out and George would wave his arms towards the still-undeveloped land and say, "This is where the office block will be and this is where the lake will be and this is where we could have concerts, etc." And here we are now and that vision is just as he described it. It was like having a father explain to his children his plans for the family. And that's what we are — a family.'

GEORGE HAD TAKEN up smoking in his late teens and was a heavy smoker for many years. Staff recall often going into his office at the winery, even for one of the early morning meetings he has always favoured, and being confronted with a grey haze of cigarette smoke. In times of stress he would revert to chain-smoking, lighting one cigarette with the remnants of an earlier one. After the trials of the receivership, his efforts to take better care of his health included many attempts to give up smoking.

After a gruelling day of meetings at a sales conference at Vidal's in 1990, George and his team were having drinks and dinner in the restaurant. During conversation George declared he was giving up smoking. Angela Lewis had heard this promise many times previously and, emboldened by a few glasses of wine, decided to challenge George. 'I said to everyone: "Let's take a bet on this. George can't give up, so it's easy money."' George was persuaded to accept a wager of $150 from each of the staff present that he couldn't go 12 months without smoking. 'That was a huge amount of money in those days, but we were so confident he could not last the distance that we thought our money was safe,' Lewis says. 'A year later George declared he had won and we handed over the money. He has never smoked since.'

But it was not to end there. A few weeks later, when the sales team was once again due to attend a conference at Vidal's, George told everyone they would be staying an extra night but did not say why. 'That night he put on the most superb degustation dinner most of us have ever had, and all of us will remember forever. There were multiple courses, each matched with the most amazing international wines like Krug, Château d'Yquem, and so on. He told us that the dinner was paid for from the money we had lost on the smoking bet. We thought it was an incredibly generous thing to do, and so like George.'

The winemaking teams at Villa Maria, Vidal and Esk Valley all came to understand that they were part of a mission, and that in George they had a pretty interesting sort of boss.

Elise Montgomery, the Vidal winemaker from 1990 to 1997, started working for George as the assistant winemaker at Villa Maria in early 1990. A Massey horticultural science and Roseworthy College graduate, she'd worked in a range of Australian, Californian and French vineyards. Her first impression of her new boss was of 'a smoke-filled office, an enormous desk and a man speaking quite possibly a foreign language sitting on the other side of it. George had been told by Kym Milne that he wanted to employ me. In the course of the interview George found out that I had a couple of other job offers, so he convinced me to take the Villa Maria job by saying "I won't pay you as much as those other wineries, but if you want to become the best winemaker you can be and learn from a great team, then this is the place for you." True to his word he did not offer nearly as much money as the others, and he did offer fantastic opportunities to grow and learn professionally. I never regretted the choice I made.'

At Villa Maria and Vidals, Montgomery found herself part of a team of young, dynamic people who were allowed to get on with things, being pushed forward as winemakers while George remained in the background. 'I recall having to lead a wine club tasting in about my second week at Villa Maria, having never done any public speaking in my life and feeling absolutely terrified as about 80 or more people filed through the door,' she says. 'It was the first of many sink-or-swim situations that Villa Maria threw at us. But we weren't left to flounder. Team dynamics were very important to George, and he was constantly checking in with each of us individually to see how the team was working.

'Over the years we went through quite a few fads. Once George gave up the cigars, it was the fitness and self-evolvement era. There was lots of walking, and even meditation training, for many of us — a skill that was very useful at times! I lost count of the number of "personality" tests we did to ascertain how we worked. One time I went to see George and told him that I thought I wanted a change of career, but I didn't know what. The next day he arranged for me to go to an employment specialist to complete aptitude tests to help me on my path. It was all very expensive and paid for by him. The results indicated that I was well suited to what I was doing, apparently, and so I stayed. I'm still not sure to this day if it was a set-up or not!'

IN 1993 ROD McDONALD was working part-time, assisting with vintage at Hotel du Vin, south of Auckland, when he saw advertised a permanent role as cellar hand at Villa Maria. He sent off his CV, along with a good word from George's old friend and associate Ian Montgomerie. Following an initial interview with Elise Montgomery and Grant Edmonds, George asked McDonald to meet him. 'I sat outside his office, nervous as hell, reading the latest Villa newsletter and trying to commit to memory the recent news and list of trophies Villa had won,' he remembers. 'I was finally invited into George's office, and two hours later I left. I then had to sit a personality test — classic Fistonich — to see what my strengths and weaknesses were. I failed that and had to re-test as I was "inconclusive". It either meant I was trying to fool the test, was a generalist or I had no personality!'

After a second hour-long interview, George offered McDonald a job working for Montgomery as cellar hand at Vidal. 'It was my first experience of George's absolute love of the minutiae of his business. There was no position lower down the ladder within a winery than cellar hand, and a winery the size of Villa back then would employ up to 20 across the country in any year. The fact that the owner of New Zealand's largest privately owned wine company would spend three hours of his time employing a cellar hand speaks volumes about George, Villa Maria and the kind of business it is.'

In 1993 Vidal was in the throes of a make-over. The atmosphere of change and improvement provided McDonald with a timely insight into how Vidal fitted into the greater Villa Maria group. 'My first couple of years in Hawke's Bay were a wonderful learning experience. I was exposed to how wineries worked by Elise, and what I learned very early on was that hard work was expected, initiative was encouraged and performance recognised . . . in a number of ways.'

McDonald says that when the team learned a visit from George was imminent, plenty of effort was put into making sure all was in order. 'George's visits were always met with a combination of flurried activity. Eventually we got everything to a state that he would be happy with, and the last-minute tidy-ups weren't needed — which just left the excitement and anticipation about what George was going to focus on this time around.'

Like so many others, McDonald remembers the importance placed on keeping up the Villa group team spirit. 'Vintage was a big excuse for a party. They were stuff of legend, with skits involving cross-dressing, imitations of George, themed group costumes, bad karaoke and questionable limericks all played out in front of an enthusiastic crowd, suitably lubricated by the sponsor's fine product. There were always stories to tell on the drive home at the end of the weekend. George's part in those parties was never as a spectator; he was seen to steal the show on a few occasions.'

In 1995 McDonald was promoted to assistant winemaker, and the same year, with George and Elise Montgomery's approval, he took time off to travel to Burgundy to participate in vintage there. 'George made sure I knew that I should make the most of the opportunity and that he expected a full report on "what the Frenchies were up to". I came back fully committed to staying with Villa and started to think about what next.'

Rod McDonald.

In 1997, again with support from both Elise Montgomery and George, and some financial support from Villa, McDonald headed to Lincoln University to complete a Postgraduate Diploma in Viticulture and Oenology. He returned to Vidal later that year to news that Montgomery was leaving to start a family.

'Elise sat me down and asked if I thought I could step up to the winemaking job, to which I replied, with a complete lack of understanding as to what that meant, yes. I then had a number of discussions with George, who decided to give me a shot at the big chair. It was a typical George-style decision. It was a risk — although not the biggest he's taken — as I was under-qualified, but I guess he knew if I couldn't get the job done it wouldn't be because of a lack of effort.' Indeed. In the nine years that followed, the small permanent winery team and vintage crews under McDonald took Vidal Chardonnay, Bordeaux reds and Syrah wines to a number of national trophies. In 2006, McDonald was named Winemaker of the Year at the Royal Easter Wine Show.

McDonald believes George's hands-on management of Villa Maria is unique. 'Whether it is sales, production, finance or whatever, George always puts himself where he thinks the need is greatest at the time. There was a well-established viticulture team, but while the personnel changed over time, as it does, the calibre of the team, and the lengths we went to produce the best wines we could, never changed. George always encouraged us to make sensible decisions about vineyards and at harvest time, but he was always the first to encourage us to take chances and think on our feet where a crop was looking better than it should or beyond our expectation. If there was a chance to make great wine and a better return, we were to take it!'

Healthy competition between Villa, Vidal and Esk for the best fruit and vineyards was encouraged, but McDonald recalls it was never excessive. 'Back then George was actively involved in the allocation of fruit between brands, as well as the group assessment and blending of our wines. It was one of the real strengths of working as part of the Villa group winemakers: that we would assess, comment, discuss, and on occasion berate, all our wines in blind line-ups of some of what went on to become some of New Zealand's greatest wines.'

McDonald acknowledges that not everyone was totally comfortable with George's demand for completely open discussion within the team. 'Often this could lead to an unnerving level of frankness, but there is no doubt it was a great forum to discuss the nuts and bolts of what was working in the vineyard and winery. It was also an incredible place to learn, and part of that learning was on occasion being humbled as we unveiled the wines and found out what we had tasted. There were never any recriminations.'

One occasion stands out for McDonald as demonstrating just how perceptive George is about wine. 'On a walk through the Vidal barrel cellar with George in my first year as winemaker, tasting Chardonnay from barriques, George was particularly taken with a couple of barrels of Chardonnay from a new grower. I told him it was a block we were pretty excited about and hoped it would become part of the Reserve wine that year. Six months later, in a line-up of 160-odd Chardonnays, the same wine came up in a blind line-up and he picked it not as from that particular grower, but as wine that had the x-factor that should be included in a Reserve wine. We did include it, and that wine went on to win the first trophy for Chardonnay we won while I was winemaker. George really knows his apples.'

McDonald is also complimentary about George's respect for initiative. 'One of the things I learned and saw others use to good effect was that George is a huge fan of making decisions, encouraging people within his business to show initiative and do their homework. That being said, he can be a nightmare if he doesn't really believe in the idea. George once told me that he had saved millions of dollars over the years by saying no to people when they came to him with requests to change things or to spend money on capital expenditure. He also said that the good ideas always came back either better researched or with someone passionate enough to fight for it. Either way, he argued, it was a better result. The bad ideas just disappeared . . .

'During my time with Vidal, I had the chance to be part of a number of different personal growth/team-building courses. George was a great believer in encouraging his people to grow, and it was often as a result of George reading a book or meeting someone he thought was inspiring or worth listening to. Some of them were a bit questionable, but some were gold. While at Vidal's, I was actively involved in the regional organisation, Hawke's Bay Winegrowers, including a stint as chairman for around five years. Our role was helping to develop Hawke's Bay's national and international brands. It was important to represent Vidal and the Villa Maria group in the role, but also it was a great opportunity to learn about what made the industry tick.

'I've never added up what that investment of my time would have cost George, but it was something he always encouraged and saw value in. He always had a larger vision for what Hawke's Bay could become if it could combine Napier and Hastings and centralise its efforts to govern and promote itself. He was a supporter of any initiative or individual who he believed was pursuing that goal.'

George describes McDonald as 'an extremely fine winemaker, with real passion and an unmatched ability for innovation. Every year Rod would make valuable improvements at Vidal's and we all benefited from those. He ran a totally clean ship and was a great mentor to those who worked with him.'

McDonald still values George's opinion, and has immense admiration for his loyalty to the people who work for him and the time he gives them. 'One thing that amazed me, and frustrated the hell out of various consultants who tried to change him, was the number of people who worked for George who would phone him regularly or whom he would ring to find out what was going on within his business. He is ridiculously busy and on occasion difficult to pin down, but he always takes or returns your call. I'm not sure if Gail would agree it's one of his strengths!'

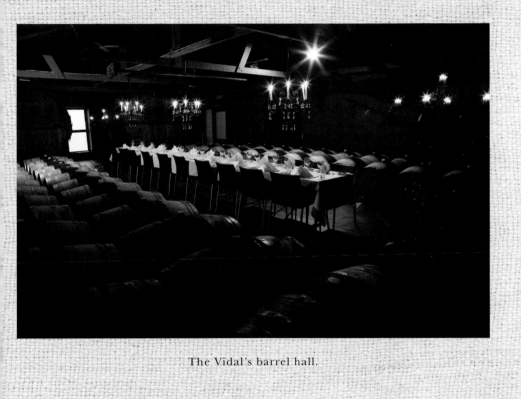

The Vidal's barrel hall.

16
OFF TO THE AWATERE

In 1992 the company was going through another expansionary phase and needed access to grapes, particularly from Marlborough, where competition for long-term contracts meant land prices were being driven even higher than in other parts of the country.

George uses the loud-hailer
to explain new plantings
at the Terra Vitae blocks
in Marlborough during an
investors' open day.

George also needed more capital. 'The simple truth is that it was increasingly difficult to get fruit or land. I was reluctant to take outside shareholders into Villa Maria, as I did not want the family ownership diluted by going even partially public. And I did not want to go back to the banks.'

The dilemma was discussed at board level, and Avon Carpenter suggested using an unlisted public company to raise the badly needed capital. 'It seemed an innovative way to get more vineyards, and after discussing the pros and cons at some length we decided to go ahead. Steve Smith, our viticulturist at the time, was tasked with finding a suitable site. He eventually identified land at Seddon, on the south side of the Awatere, as being available and suitable. It was 100 acres, and in 1992 that was a huge vineyard — with the exception of Montana there weren't many producers that had vineyards of over 100 acres. Today vineyards of 200 to 300 acres are quite common.'

Using a combination of brokers and advertising in the *National Business Review*, George went to the market. 'Our aim was to get 400 shareholders to put in $5000 each to raise $2 million. It was slow-going and we struggled, probably because a vineyard company with no wine was such a new concept. Eventually we got to $1,650,000 — $350,000 short — so we had to issue some Villa Maria rights. A finance company in Christchurch brokered them for us and we finally just made it. It was quite a stressful time.'

They named the company Seddon Vineyards, and it ran successfully from 1992 to 2005. It had its own management board (Ross Goodin, president of New Zealand Grape Growers, was appointed chairman) and operated separately from Villa Maria, although Villa Maria had an exclusive 50-year supply and vineyard management contract with Seddon.

'The shareholders seemed satisfied. They were kept informed via regular newsletters about how the company was doing; we had shareholders' field days with food and wine each year, and they received a small dividend. Plus they got special wine offers at preferential rates four times a year. Meanwhile the value of the investment was increasing as demand for vineyard land and grapes continued to increase.'

The establishment of this separate public company to buy and own vineyards that could provide Villa Maria with a consistent supply of grapes was another significant innovation for the company. The business model that Villa adopted was at the time unique in New Zealand, and its success has spawned followers.

BY 1997, WHEN Villa's increasing global exports were creating a demand for more grapes than contractors were able to supply, George decided to re-think his strategy. The obvious path would have been for Seddon Vineyards to look for more land to buy, but this would have been a complicated business process as the initial model did not take this into consideration. So rather than expanding Seddon, George decided to set up a separate company along similar lines.

'We knew of 80 hectares in Taylors Pass, on the north side of the Awatere in Marlborough, that was available. In Hawke's Bay, land that would become the Keltern Vineyard, east of Maraekakaho, and land in the heart of Gimblett Gravels that would become the Twyford Gravels Vineyard, were also an option — for a price. In 1998, 170 additional vineyard hectares was an extremely big purchase, and we knew that it would be expensive. But we needed that sort of scale to meet our projected future growth.'

An aerial view of
Villa Maria's vineyards
in the Gimblett Gravels
area of Hawke's Bay.

With board approval, George established Terra Vitae Vineyards Ltd using exactly the same model as the Seddon Vineyards venture, but as a totally separate entity. He went back to the market again, this time to seek $9.5 million. 'We realised it was a huge risk, but the difference was that we had established our credibility as a brand and we were much more confident. Seddon took almost one year, but Terra Vitae happened in about five weeks and proved to be an easy sell because we'd established a successful track record with Seddon. The offer ended up being over-subscribed, and by 1998 we had raised $13 million. We decided to send $3.5 million back as we had capped the amount; however, in retrospect we would have been better to keep it and ask the investors if we could invest in more land.'

The Hawke's Bay vineyards were subsequently planted in Merlot, Cabernet Franc, Cabernet Sauvignon, Syrah, Pinot Noir, Chardonnay, Gewürztraminer and Sémillon, which provided George with a significant increase in the supply of the varieties he was so eager to gain. The Taylors Pass vineyard was to supply further high-quality Sauvignon Blanc, with smaller parcels of Riesling, Chardonnay, Pinot Gris and Pinot Noir.

IN 2005, SEDDON and Terra Vitae, both fully established and operating successfully, were merged into a single company, although the vineyards themselves are still operated under their individual names: Seddon Vineyard, Keltern, Twyford Gravels and Taylors Pass. There were two reasons for the amalgamation. Running two separate companies took a lot of administration; one made more sense. And whereas initially they were vastly different in output, over time the similarities grew and amalgamation became easier in terms of both administration and how they fitted into the Villa Group's operations.

'The public shareholders of Terra Vitae to a large extent are wine lovers and supporters of Villa Maria,' says George. 'We still have shareholder wine tastings and barbecues in one of the vineyards every year, and we send out quarterly newsletters written by the managers. They do a presentation every year, too, and in this way we keep the shareholders involved. It's a good company that goes very well and has been instrumental in Villa Maria's ability to have a consistent, long-term source of grapes.'

Terra Vitae has its own board: Milan Brajkovich (husband of George's daughter Karen), who is a viticulturist; Andrew Pearson, a stock broker; and a professional director and farmer from Marlborough, Joe Ferraby, who is the current chairman. George sits on the board representing the 25 per cent shareholding owned by Villa Maria and the Fistonich family. Both he and Brajkovich remove themselves from all decisions where any conflict of interest may be perceived, such as contract pricing.

Karen Fistonich recalls the setting up of Seddon Vineyards as a very interesting time for the Villa board. It was the first time, effectively, that the board had been involved in a project that was distinct from the usual board governance. 'Rather than this being just one of Dad's projects requiring a rubber stamp, board members this time were very much involved in sorting out the structure to be used and getting the prospectus organised and approved. The process went well; there were lots of extra meetings around that time, to sort out the constitution and all the matters that go with that.'

The success of the Terra Vitae project posed another dilemma for George: how to process all the extra grapes that would be coming Villa Maria's way. Villa Maria had been taking fruit from Marlborough since the late 1980s, and, as volumes increased, having control of processing close to the source of the grapes was essential for maintaining and improving quality. George was also very aware of the long-term benefits of wine tourism, and was determined to select a winery site that would help enhance the brand image.

The search began for a suitable site, with viticulturist Steve Smith canvassing the options. In 1996, a site in Blenheim on the corner of New Renwick Road and Paynters Road was selected, close to the Wairau vineyards and the airport, and with spectacular views over both the Richmond Ranges and Wither Hills. It was also an advantage that the site adjoined a golf course.

George was already very busy with other projects, and he felt he needed someone who could drive the project. He approached his nephew, Fabian Yukich, who had worked with him once before. Yukich had left Villa Maria in the late 1970s to work for his father, Frank, at Montana and Penfolds, before attending Roseworthy Wine College in South Australia. He spent time working in the Australian wine industry and then came home to New Zealand, working as project site manager during the construction of the new Penfolds winery in Gisborne. Fabian had been out of the wine industry for a number of years and was keen to return. For his part, George knew that in his nephew he had someone with wine-industry and building experience whom he could trust to get the job done.

Yukich joined the company in March 1998, on contract for a year or until the new winery was complete. Yukich soon discovered there was plenty to be done. 'At this stage planning was in its early stages,' he remembers. 'There had been sketches done and there were initial capacity calculations and overall concepts but more detail was needed.

'George had an expectation that everything would be complete in time for the 1999 vintage, but they hadn't appointed an architect, an engineer or a builder, so the first thing I had to do was get that organised.'

George needed an architect with a vision for a building that would be in scale with the landscape and have a sense of presence. He had seen the work that Hamish Cameron of Archimedia had done for Michael Brajkovich at Kumeu River Wines, and had checked out his other commercial work, and was impressed with how Cameron could make a building work in its landscape. George was clear about what he wanted: predominantly New Zealand materials and a New Zealand design. He did not want a 'pretend-French' or 'pretend-European' appearance. A project team was put together, including George, Yukich, landscape designer Jo Saunders, and structural engineer the late Mike Brading. This would be the same team that would plan and build the new Auckland winery just three years later.

George gave his nephew plenty of responsibility, but insisted that Yukich ensure the new facility was capable of meeting future needs. 'George said to me, "I want you to work out how big we are going to be in 50 years' time and I want you to design a winery that will still meet our needs then." So I went back 20 years and looked at the year-on-year growth, and then using those rates, plus some, we worked out what we would potentially need. I drew all that up and that cemented our thinking about how we would lay the place out.'

Yukich worked with the viticulturists, winemakers, cellar hands, trucking companies and contractors to develop a winery design that would totally focus on wine quality and efficient processing from the moment the trucks carrying the grapes entered the winery gates. George insisted that Yukich spend time travelling to other wineries in New Zealand, Australia and Europe, and to trade exhibitions in Europe, to learn the very latest in wine technology.

As with all projects, there would be many changes. 'I would meet with George very regularly to discuss progress, and he would say, "Let's move that over there a little bit . . .", and there were always minor things to be changed here and there in terms of layout,' Yukich remembers. 'I had started by doing drawings of what the winery should look like, but I became conscious of re-doing things by hand all the time, so I bought a CAD programme and began teaching myself how to use it. Then we could tweak the plans in an instant and pass them on to the architect and engineers.'

One of the key objectives of the project was to be environmentally responsible. Yukich asked refrigeration engineer the late Allan McCreadie to look at how the waste heat from the refrigeration plant could be recovered and used for energy in the winemaking process. At the time such equipment was rare in the wine industry, and when Yukich did the initial payback analysis he was disappointed to find that on current volumes the equipment would take 16 to 17 years to recover the investment. The project went ahead anyway. From a long-term view it still made sense, and as it turned out power prices increased steadily, as did the size of the winery. Recovered energy now makes up the majority of the heat needed for warming ferments at the Marlborough and the Auckland wineries, and the financials are much more favourable given the scale of the business and increasing power costs.

The winery processes all of Villa Maria's Marlborough grapes, as well

DROUGH

The Villa Maria
winery on New
Renwick Road,
near Blenheim.
The Wither Hills
are in the distance.

as some from Waipara and Nelson. 'It's grown a lot since we opened it,' says Yukich. 'The building and the winery were absolutely state-of-the-art at time of opening, and, because the design makes it easy to expand and develop, we have been able to allow for new technologies that we couldn't have foreseen even with our meticulous planning.'

SIX MONTHS AFTER Yukich joined the company, Villa Maria's operations manager Peter Groves left. Yukich looked at the role and decided to apply; it would be a full-time job. 'So I went to George, but he didn't give me an either-or option: he said I could probably do both jobs at the same time!' So it was that Yukich became operations manager, overseeing bottling, quality and distribution, and national wineries infrastructure manager.

By this time the winery at Kirkbride Road that George had built in the 1970s was stretched to its limits. Although it was on a six-hectare site, it was severely constrained at the boundaries, and the land George had purchased to expand his original vineyard was not that suitable for winery expansion. Although Yukich worked on a number of options for rebuilding on the site, George was already saying that the company should not preclude the option of moving. In 1999 George and Yukich, with the encouragement of Manukau City mayor Sir Barry Curtis, began exploring other sites in the Manukau region. Again George wanted a site that had a sense of presence, one that would be a headquarters winery with a unique New Zealand feel about it, and enhance an image of quality.

During the search for land, George, Yukich and architect Hamish Cameron inadvertently wandered onto land on Oruarangi Road. As they looked down into the bowl of a volcanic crater, Waitomokia, George remarked, 'That looks like a pretty good site for a winery.' From the ridge there were views of the Manukau Harbour, and, although now somewhat overgrown, there were a number of stands of mature trees that must have at one point been planted to a plan. It looked like a good location. And the location close to Auckland airport was highly strategic. Unfortunately it was not for sale, and the tenant of the warehouse that sat on one edge of the property had just renewed the lease.

It took nine months of negotiation with the landowner and the lessee to secure a purchase at terms that all parties thought favourable. In August 2000, Villa Maria took possession of the initial 67-acre block, later expanding this to 100 acres to secure its boundaries. Work started almost immediately, with Yukich hiring his cousins Ivan and Tony Yukich to do the land-clearing for the vineyard. Ivan and Tony were sons of the late Mate Yukich, for whom George had once worked in the early years of Montana Wines.

George convinced Drazen Mijatov — a talented viticulturist who was at the time already busy setting up the Keltern Vineyard in the Hawke's Bay and a plant nursery — to work with Jo Saunders to plan and plant the vineyard, while Yukich once again worked with the winemakers and George to establish the flow of the winery. It was important to keep in mind that the winery was also a retail outlet and events centre. Aesthetics were critical.

As all this was going on, George commissioned artist Cynthia Taylor to do a representation of what the winery in the volcanic crater could look like. He jokes that the painting was a lot more meaningful than drawing up a business plan for the development, with line-by-line costings. 'We knew how much we wanted to spend and that was adequate,' he says. 'Whenever anyone asks to see the plan for the new winery I just show them the painting.' The engineering, architecture and landscape design team that worked on the Marlborough winery re-formed to plan out what was to be a $30 million project that would go on to win two architecture awards, again with a blueprint for expansion over the next 50 years.

Planting the vineyard, landscaping the grounds, and building the winery was an exciting time. Every decision about the winery design had to be examined in terms of the impact on wine quality and how it would work in terms of the long-term plan. George was more than ever determined that, in however many years, a lack of forethought would not mean that the original design would be compromised by ad hoc add-ons.

The Villa Maria
winery, company
head office and
function centre
in Mangere.

Prime Minister
Helen Clark declares
the new Auckland
winery open.

Environmental considerations also played a big part. Substantial heat-recovery infrastructure was built into the engineering design of the winery. The warehouse featured a night-air cooling system, and all the buildings capitalised on the use of natural light. Instead of carting waste from the demolished buildings to a landfill, the concrete was crushed on-site and reused as base course. Timber from the buildings was used for improvements to the Kirkbride Road site, which remained in partial use until 2005.

During the resource consent process Yukich established contact with the Makaurau Marae, one of the oldest continuous inhabitations of Maori people in the region. Working with the late Danny Roberts, the environmental representative of the marae, sparked Villa Maria's commitment to go to additional lengths to ensure that stormwater from the driveways and car parks would be filtered through a series of underground weirs before leaving the property and flowing into the Oruarangi Creek, and ultimately into the recently cleaned-up Manukau Harbour.

Danny's wife, Irene, had worked at Villa Maria in the 1970s, and the couple had often played in the band that entertained at the winery. In recent times Danny and Irene's children and grandchildren had been part of a kapa haka cultural performance at a winery open day that also featured traditional Croatian dancing.

The board of Villa Maria invited the marae committee to discuss the plans, and an arrangement was made for kaumatua Maurice Wilson to be present and perform a blessing at the commencement of each stage of the construction. These blessings became important milestones in the development of the winery. During each blessing ceremony, all work stopped, and everybody on-site joined in. On a number of occasions Sir Barry Curtis attended, as did Villa Maria board members. When the administration block opened, Maurice performed the blessing for the last time during the construction phase. His prayer in Maori, with members of the marae joining in the singing, was responded to in Maori by Villa Maria staff, with long-time employee Issac King taking the lead. They were emotional occasions, with the Villa Maria directors moved to tears at the final one.

Maurice Wilson was also present to perform the blessing at the official opening of the winery in 2005 by Prime Minister Helen Clark.

GEORGE HAD ALWAYS supported the local community — the community in which he has spent his entire life — and the move to the new winery brought with it new opportunities to be involved. Fabian Yukich served on the steering group for the Mangere Heritage Trail, and through this George became aware of plans to industrialise large areas of untouched rural land with significant heritage value. George was appalled by how environmentally and aesthetically unsound the plans were, and Villa Maria put considerable effort into helping the local community successfully fight plans to put factories on the shores of the harbour, his childhood playground.

The Cynthia Taylor painting *Oruarangi
Road*, which George commissioned to
hang in the new winery. It shows the
gentle Manukau Harbour coastline
around which he has spent all his life.

17
INDUSTRY
LEADER

There were major differences in scale between the largest four wine companies and the rest, leading to a variety of operating styles. That was understandable. But what George and several other small companies found really frustrating was a key area where there was a lack of synergy — the quality of cork and its spoiling impact, and a determination to find an alternative.

George Fistonich makes his
point. The photo received
world-wide exposure in the
wine media.

R uined wine was an issue affecting the vast majority of wine producers, and with annual wine exports to the United Kingdom, the United States and Australia approaching the 23-million-litre mark, it was a problem that needed addressing. In 2001 a group of quality-focused wine producers initiated the Marlborough Screwcap Initiative to promote the use of screwcap seals on wines.

This quickly became the New Zealand Screwcap Initiative, with many members replacing cork with screwcaps on their lower-level wines. But George was to go much further. 'By the time 2000 rolled around we simply could not get enough decent cork. It was a problem that had been developing for some years, but it reached a point for us where we were losing a minimum 8 per cent to bad cork. For a number of years we were taking statistical random samples from bales of 10,000 corks and soaking them in individual glasses of neutral white wine or distilled water overnight to see how good the bales were. We were rejecting three to five out of every ten bales and sending them back to our local suppliers. There was a belief in the wine industry that many of these bales didn't make it back to Portugal but were on-sold to smaller companies without the infrastructure to test their quality.

'Our whole objective was to make quality wine, so the decision to convert to 100 per cent screwcap took about half an hour. We weren't the only ones. In Marlborough alone there were about 15

George with nurseryman Drazen Mijatov in the Villa Maria
nursery in Hawke's Bay. George had first met Drazen when
he was working as a cleaner at Villa Maria's Auckland winery.
George discovered that Drazen was in fact a highly qualified
viticulturist and so gave him a job in the nursery. Later the two
went into the grape-plant supply business together.

Drazen's wife, Tehana, runs New Zealand's only certified
wine-virus testing labratory.

or 20 of us. Only the limited initial access to caps and bottles slowed the switch down. In 2001 we started doing the 2000-vintage reds, and in 2002 we told the world that from then on all wines under the Villa Maria, Vidal, and Esk Valley brands would be closed with screwcaps. We were the first major winery in the world to make such a total commitment. To make our point we declared ourselves a cork-free zone.'

Not all of George's sales staff were convinced this was the right move. Angela Lewis, who was in charge of trade marketing, recalls plenty of dissension. 'When George decided to put our Reserve and Single Vineyard wines under screwcap first, some around here thought he had gone completely crazy. Shortly after he announced what was happening, one woman burst into the area where the sales team sat and said "Is he completely mad?" But George took the view that he knew real wine enthusiasts — that is, those who bought our premium wines — were sick of cork-tainted or oxidised wine, so they would be the easiest to convince and they would form a vanguard for convincing others. It was really another George masterstroke that shows the strength of his intuition when it comes to wine.'

Terry Dunleavy, former chief executive of New Zealand Winegrowers and a highly influential personality in the modern New Zealand wine industry, believes George's decision on the matter of screwcaps is a vintage example of his dedication to high-quality wine excellence. 'In 2001, when the wine world was still debating the merits of screwcaps as wine closures, George made what was an incredibly bold decision, but one that confirmed the Villa Maria group's dedication not just to innovation, but to assuring wine lovers of absolute protection of the unique intensity of grape flavours for which New Zealand has since become known internationally,' he says.

Shortly afterwards George travelled to the United Kingdom, where his trade sub-distributor Matthew Clark was holding a sales conference attended by around 300 sales reps. George was asked to address them, and he took the opportunity to raise the issue of screwcaps. He arrived at the meeting armed with a copy of a book, launched the previous day, by eminent wine writer Hugh Johnson, who opined that 'if screwcaps were available 100 years ago imagine all the fantastic wines we would now be drinking'.

'I asked the reps how many believed in screwcaps. From the show of hands it looked to me that something like 35 per cent were for them while the rest were against. So I read out what Johnson had said. I also had a video that we played, and by the end of my 20 minutes I think we managed to convert another 30 per cent of them.'

Like others in the industry, George understood that the American market would be the most difficult to convert. They resolved to be fully prepared to deal with any backlash by responding quickly to any negativity. 'The size of the market and the importance it has for us meant that finding ways to gain their acceptance of screwcaps was imperative. In the beginning we received dozens and dozens of letters.' One that George recalls came from an expatriate New Zealander. 'He said, "I've lived in America for 10 years, and I have been proud of the New Zealand wine industry, but I am ashamed about Villa Maria trying to destroy the great reputation of New Zealand wine by using screwcaps."'

The office administrators at Villa Maria were instructed that every letter had to be answered immediately. 'So first thing every morning a team would open the mail and send a pre-prepared letter thanking people for their concern, then explaining why we were changing. Then we offered to provide them with a personal copy of a more detailed 20-page document that set out the science behind the decision. And we engaged them by saying how obvious it was that they were really passionate about wine. It worked. We had an equal number of letters from people writing thanking us for the prompt response and explanation. More importantly, most of them said they understood our reasoning and would be supporting the move to screwcaps. They became ambassadors for our decision.'

Local consumers were, in fact, relatively relaxed about the change. 'I received one letter saying, "I've been drinking your wine for the last 20 years. My wife and I sit down every night with a meal and have a nice glass of wine. Unfortunately, because you have gone to screwcaps I'll never be able to drink your wine again. Thank you for the great time I have had with your wine over the last 20 years. I used to be able to get home, get the corkscrew out and open the bottle, sit down and pour myself a glass of wine. Now I get home and my wife has worked out how to take the screwcap off and she has already finished the bottle, and is incapable of cooking my meal. So I've had to ban screwcaps."'

Villa Maria has a long-held objective to be environmentally responsible and to operate using sustainable practices. In 1999, the company launched its organics programme, and it now has four BioGro-certified vineyard blocks and others in transition. Nearly a third of the company-owned vineyards are organically managed. Additionally, all Villa Maria wineries and vineyards are certified under the Sustainable Winegrowing New Zealand (SWNZ) accreditation, introduced by a large group of New Zealand winegrowers to set environmental standards for their industry. In 2009 the company convinced New Zealand glass manufacturer O-I Glass to manufacture lighter-weight glass bottles, and it has been using these since February 2010. In 2010 Fabian Yukich won the Sustainability Champion Award at the New Zealand Sustainable Business Network Awards. And in June 2012 the Minister for the Environment presented Fabian Yukich with the Supreme Green Ribbon Award in recognition of the company's contribution to protecting the New Zealand environment.

GEORGE IS OPTIMISTIC that the New Zealand wine industry will survive and grow, but in a frank interview with an English publication in mid-2011 he pointed to changes in the industry that he clearly sees as problematic. 'I know there is a lot of talk about a wine surplus and some are looking to blame specific companies, but some of the blame lies with the speculators, often — but not always — big corporations, who came into the industry hoping to make a quick dollar, based on all the hard work the long-term players had been doing for over 30 years to build brand New Zealand in the overseas markets.'

If this criticism seems incongruous coming from someone who

has always believed in the need for constant growth, the defence is that it is an issue of quality. 'Our business has more or less doubled in size over the past 10 to 12 years, while in the same period some of the multinationals and speculators have gone from almost nothing to up to three times our size. They have not built premium brands over a period of time. So what do they do? They flood the market with cheap and bulk wine that lowers the image of all New Zealand wine. What they don't realise is that the wine business is a long-term proposition. You cannot turn supply off and on like a tap, as you can in beverage industries, and the weather can always wipe away the year's profits. A lot of these players get into the industry, do a heap of damage to the country's brand, then get out or sell when they realise that it's not about short-term profit.'

Understanding and dealing with exchange-rate fluctuations across the many markets Villa deals in is a skill George never thought he would need when he started out with five acres of grapes. 'It can have a massive impact on the business, and we put a lot of effort into managing our currency risk. Even so the situation in the UK, which is our biggest market, is challenging at the moment with the low value of the pound. You used to get NZ$3 to the pound; now — 2012 — it is about $1.90. With the supermarkets and their promotional costs, the profit in the UK is virtually non-existent. I'd hate to have been in this situation 15 years ago when our brand was not as well known as it is today.

'We have built up quite a lot of equity in Villa Maria, and we have also built up a spread of around 50 markets around the world, including Russia and India. We are in the USA, Canada, Australia, Asia. Villa Maria now supplies a number of the large international chains and, importantly, has wines in prestigious restaurants around the world. So we can weather the storm, but it is hard-going. We have been hit with the huge 2011 harvest surplus at the same time as fewer routes to market, as well as an unfavourable exchange rate. I think I have worked harder than ever the last couple of years.

'It is an odd situation at the moment. On the one hand you have family businesses like Villa Maria, and the other wine companies that promote themselves with us as 'The Family of Twelve', where the owners are connected to the land and the making of the wine. That brings real diversity to the wines and value to the country's image and brand. On the other hand you have the multinationals with huge investments and economies of scale, and then on top of that has grown this phenomenon of the "virtual brand", where the wine is made from contracted grapes, made in a contracted winery, often bottled thousands of kilometres away, and sometimes with a name that misleads you into thinking there is an individual behind it. From my perspective, the problem with those models is that wine gets treated like any other beverage: it becomes a homogeneous, bland blend with no real personality, no connection to the land, no soul.'

IT HAD ALWAYS been George's intention that Villa Maria stay in family ownership. With a background in banking and a strong interest in the wine business, Karen, George and Gail's eldest child, was the logical family member to assist George by taking on responsibility for ensuring the family's interests remained well-represented. She joined the board of Villa Maria as a director in 1992, and became chair of the board in 2006.

Karen, who has a BA in Psychology, joined the ANZ bank on its graduate programme after university. She is married to Milan Brajkovich, a member of the highly regarded winemaking family from Kumeu, west of Auckland. In the late 1980s, when Karen was in her late twenties, export was becoming a major part of the Villa Maria business and George was starting to travel more. On one occasion George and Gail were going overseas for six weeks, and Karen, who was working at an ANZ branch not far from the airport, went out to farewell her parents. Unexpectedly, George handed Karen the keys to his filing cabinet and gave her a briefing on who in the leadership group of the company she could rely on, as well as a bit of a rundown on their personalities.

'He thought very, very highly of the senior winemaker Kym Milne. Dad had total confidence in Kym's ability,' she remembers. 'He gave me his opinion on the other senior leaders at the time, what their

Villa Maria board chairman
Karen Fistonich and her father
in the vineyard at Mangere.

relative strengths were and which parts of the business they were involved with. He talked about Ian Clark, because he has always thought Ian is good at what he does. He said another strong leader was Steve Smith, senior viticulturist at the time, and there must have been somebody who was in charge of sales.'

Karen was taken by surprise by her father's candour. Until then he had never spoken to Karen about taking any kind of role. A year later the same thing happened; prior to leaving for overseas, George gave Karen another quick briefing, a pattern that was to be repeated on every departure. 'He soon realised this was not a viable way of preparing me for any unexpected eventuality,' she explains, 'and that if the plane went down he needed someone in the family to know in more depth what was happening in the business.'

Occasionally Karen had considered becoming more involved in the company, but hadn't really seen a role for herself. 'I wasn't a winemaker, I wasn't a viticulturist, I wasn't a sales rep, and so I didn't know where I would fit into what was then a very simple business with quite defined roles.'

But clearly George, even in those early days, had identified that there was a need for somebody in the family to be familiar with the business. In 1991, after discussing the matter with Avon Carpenter and Ian Montgomerie, and with advisor Peter Howell, who thought Karen's banking background would add value, George suggested to Karen that she join the board.

'Initially my reaction was, "Well, okay, I'll come and observe." He said, "No, you have to be part of the decision-making process and be a proper director."'

Karen was initially sensitive about what her brother, Michael, and her mother would think of this show of confidence in her. 'I don't know if my mother really understood how much she contributed behind the scenes, but she seemed genuinely excited at the prospect that I could get involved. Dad broached the subject with my brother, and I've broached it with him as well. I think now all our memories are a bit fuzzy about it, because we've all got slightly different takes, but my brother has always been very computer-orientated and not so much business-orientated, at least not in the conventional sense. I always got the impression, too, that he looks at Dad's lifestyle and Dad's whole life at the winery and thinks that's not the way he wants his life to be, and I think he was quite happy at the time that I took the role. Michael has good balance between work and recreational activities, and now as a father he spends a lot of time doing the father-son thing. He hadn't really shown any interest in the wine business, but then a few years later he made some homemade wine with our cousin Fabian [Yukich]. Although Michael enjoyed making the homemade wine for a few years, he has commented to me since that solving computer technical problems holds more challenge and interest.'

As it happened, Gail, with a few reservations, endorsed George's decision. 'Both Karen and Michael worked at the winery in the university holidays. Karen would work in the wine shop, and she and George used to have reasonably vigorous debates as to how the wine shop should be run, so I was curious how the dynamic would work. But with Michael it would have been too big a clash of personalities. If Michael made a mistake George took a very hard line.

'It would have been like going back to when George was pottering around the winery at the same time as his father was pottering, and there was a clash there. It was a natural clash between father and son — that Croatian thing happening again. It simply wouldn't have worked.'

Karen was briefed by the company secretary before her first meeting, and governance was discussed. She remembers that George told her, 'It's the most interesting board I've ever been on. You'll find it fascinating, the personalities involved and the lively debate.'

'And it was interesting,' she says. 'You did get fiery debates. But it was definitely a lot simpler then, and I have noticed over time how as the business has become more complex the board has become more formal. The board was formally constituted and there was a certain liability on the directors, but there has been a shift over time, and governance has shifted to where people are now very aware of their directorial responsibilities. Back then it operated more as an advisory panel for Dad. He would bring issues to the table and everyone would give their opinion or give advice, and Peter Howell and Avon Carpenter might disagree on something and have what seemed like a fiery debate, and then Dad would go away and make his own decision. In those days it wasn't a decision-making board. My father, as the principal shareholder, held and wielded all the decision-making power.'

Understandably, Karen felt somewhat daunted at the first board meeting. 'I was female and younger; they were male, two were over 50, and all were very experienced. No one was afraid to speak their minds at the meetings, but they were always courteous and professional. And they all said they'd mind their Ps and Qs for me, so it didn't take me long to get comfortable. It was a good environment, and a good learning curve.'

At first Karen, feeling that she didn't have much to offer, took a passive role. 'There was nothing that I thought I needed to change urgently. My banking background meant that when it came to foreign-exchange risks and protection I certainly was equipped to contribute to any discussion. Avon Carpenter and I would be strong advocates for protection; the rest of the board would try to be a bit more conservative and risk-averse. Dad was more of a risk-taker. You couldn't really keep the reins on Dad, but you'd always admire his confidence.'

IN THE EARLY and mid-1990s the Villa Maria board was fully mindful of its fiduciary obligations and directorial responsibilities. 'You could tell the board was thinking there was a certain amount of risk around with Dad taking on more debt to finance a vineyard or building a new facility. But he always sold it as an educated, informed analysis built on intuitive knowledge from being in the industry for a long time. We often felt that we were heading in the right direction, but were not always comfortable with the level of risk attached.'

Although he was a financial advisor to the board rather than a director, during the 20 years of his involvement with the company Peter Howell retained a good deal of influence. 'We treated Peter like a director. He was always watching the risk and watching the cash flow and watching the debt levels, and providing a very strong counsel to the board and Dad as required,' says Karen.

'I was an accountant who happened to also be an advisor,' says Howell. 'My role was to represent the financial aspect of what the company was doing, but just how much influence I had on George is difficult to say. I listened to George. George didn't much tolerate views of opposition.'

Howell echoes Karen Fistonich's description of George's domination of the board. 'Things would come to the table, were discussed, and then George would go and make his decision. I don't recall any issues that were so significant that if George and I had disagreed it could have resulted in my stepping away. George is a very powerful person who retains all effective power. George's involvement in, and attachment to, Villa Maria is all-consuming, and in my mind may be equal to his attachment to his family. In other words, Villa Maria is a totally vital part of his life, the same as it is for anyone who has fought so hard to establish something. He is totally dedicated to the company he developed.

'He was and is very experienced, an expert in every facet of the business. He has grown the grapes; he's made the wine; he's sold the wine — and he knows it all. I say this in the most complimentary way: it's not that he thinks he knows it all; he genuinely *does* know the industry through and through. Which perhaps worked almost to the detriment of Villa Maria, because no matter who is doing what within the company, George knows more about the job than they do, and I am sure that's true. He does.'

The make-up of the Villa Maria board has changed only occasionally over the years. Avon Carpenter (now deceased), Steve Bridges, Ian Montgomerie and Peter Howell have now all retired, but were active on the board for many years. Howell was replaced by Scotsman Rob Aitken, ex-Pernod Ricard, who had a background in both the wine and financial industries. He retired a couple of years ago from

Karen and George Fistonich.

the board to pursue other projects in Scotland.

Today the board comprises George, Karen Fistonich as chair, consultant Mike Pratt, and George's nephew Fabian Yukich, who joined in 2006. Recently Sue Clark, who joined Villa Maria as sales manager in 1998 and spent around four years in that role before setting up as a sales consultant, joined the board as an advisor.

'Notwithstanding the strong personalities, the board has always worked well,' says Karen. 'There have never been any major issues where the board or Dad and I have really struggled to find agreement. It's always been the sort of board that can come to a unanimous decision. It's not as if every decision has to come to a vote.'

George, in fact, welcomed the challenge he'd occasionally face from Peter Howell and Avon Carpenter. 'Peter in particular became my mentor, and I found myself thriving with his style. It gives me no particular pleasure to always have my own way. I like to be made to think about my plans and to have to argue for them.' George sees a quiet authority in his daughter. She's heavily involved in community work, fundraising for school sports teams and the like, just as he was.

The relationship between George and Karen can, however, involve a degree of frustration. 'Our father-daughter dynamic sometimes gets a bit tricky, because he's always done it his way and I might have an alternative view, so we butt heads every now and then. Often if I challenge him he will disagree with me. We both get frustrated and I will be about to tear my hair out, then the next day he'll have changed his mind and agree with me, and I'll think to myself, that was easier than I thought it was going to be.

'Dad has great attention to detail, which is a strength as well as sometimes meaning that he does micro-manage, and I do have debates with him about how involved in minor matters he is. Sometimes he pulls back, but this need to be totally informed and his attention to making sure things are done correctly underpins the focus on quality which has always been his mantra for the company.

According to Karen Fistonich, Villa Maria is currently in very good shape. 'It's robust, with a solid foundation. You can't deny it's a challenging environment. There's always a challenge, every year

— whether it's grape supply, or the exchange rate, or the pricing. It seems that since the global financial crisis we've had every challenge on the table at once, and it can seem a bit unfair, but in the end it's pleasing to see that, because the foundation is strong and it's a strong brand, we're surviving comfortably.'

AS GEORGE ENTERS his early seventies, succession is a topic that exercises Karen and others intimately associated with the company. 'Further growth is more about being big enough to look after the company's overseas markets and be significant enough to earn our position on supermarket shelves and on the wine lists of the various wine outlets. Growth remains a goal, but the clear desire is that any expansion is measured, especially of the distribution network and the overseas markets. The company approach is that growth must also be measured by quality enhancement in everything Villa Maria does, particularly in staff satisfaction and innovation, as that is the recipe for a sustainable future.' The generally held view is that George is quite capable of continuing to spearhead Villa's growth for a further few years, but in 2011, in anticipation of his stepping gradually away from day-to-day management, efforts to strengthen the top level leadership team within the business began. As Karen comments, 'Last year my focus was largely on co-creating a new management structure for Villa Maria to help take us forward. Through feedback from the senior leadership team and invaluable assistance from Mike Pratt we strengthened our top leadership team by adding a new position of general manager commercial to help release Dad from some of his operational duties. Fortunately Dad was very receptive.'

The new general manager, Rob Ferguson, is at a level equivalent to Alastair Maling (general manager winemaking and viticulture) and Fabian Yukich (executive director wineries and vineyards) Ferguson, Maling and Yukich report directly to George, and it is to them that George can delegate many of his day-to-day duties, leaving him free to travel in the increasingly important role of brand ambassador.

George at the new
Auckland winery.

'Because he's been so busy, some frustration was setting in,' says Karen. 'There are always people wanting access to him. There are increasing demands on his time for travel and giving presentations. This is inevitable when you are the face of the company, the entrepreneur, the owner and the ultimate decision-maker. But there still has to be time and access for decision-making and consultation and feedback.'

It is not the first time Villa Maria has been down this path. Twice before, there were moves to employ both a general manager and a chief executive. 'Maybe we were looking for someone too general or maybe we couldn't quite get the job spec right,' Karen continues. 'But in essence I don't think Dad could find George No 2. So we didn't progress. At that time he wasn't really ready to let go of the reins, but he is beginning to realise that it's time to start progressively letting other people pick up some of the workload. He remains as chief executive, but he's able to let go more of his operational duties so he can focus more on the big picture.'

Karen and others believe George still has much to contribute. 'He has that vision and that big-picture view, and he thinks so strategically. Being a lateral thinker as well, we can't let him go just yet, and he wouldn't want to let go. It's a progression, and the next year or so is probably the start of that.'

But while he may realise this is the time to strengthen the leadership of the company so he is free to focus on where to add most value, George is not going to find it easy to remove himself from the front line.

'He probably won't ever fully retire,' says Karen. 'He'll always be involved, and it's just finding the way that he can be most productively involved. When he was 60, we sat around the table at our bach in Waipu and said, "You're 60 now, Dad, and you should be thinking about when you're going to retire", and he nodded and said "Sixty-five". That sort of came and went and now he's probably in that space again where he's saying, "Oh well, yeah, maybe 75", but he's not silly enough now to put an age on it.'

As the nature of George's involvement changes, and as he becomes less involved in the day-to-day running of the company, Karen is assuming more and more responsibility. 'People are always asking me about the succession, and asking, "Well, are you going to do it, Karen?" And I say, "Well, I don't have to be the managing director within the business, because the family perspective can come through the board and the leadership team can take care of the day-to-day operational side."

'But on the other side of things that's why I've become much more closely involved recently. As I am the family successor, I've had a bit of time to get used to that role, being on the board for a long while. I think that Dad had a lot of foresight in this. He got me involved while I was still relatively young. It was a good way to do it, a demonstration of just how forward-thinking he is.'

As for George, he says that a complex, modern company can no longer be run by one dominating figure. Senior leadership teams and a strong board are the way of the future. The one-man-band has to become the team leader.

18
THE FUTURE

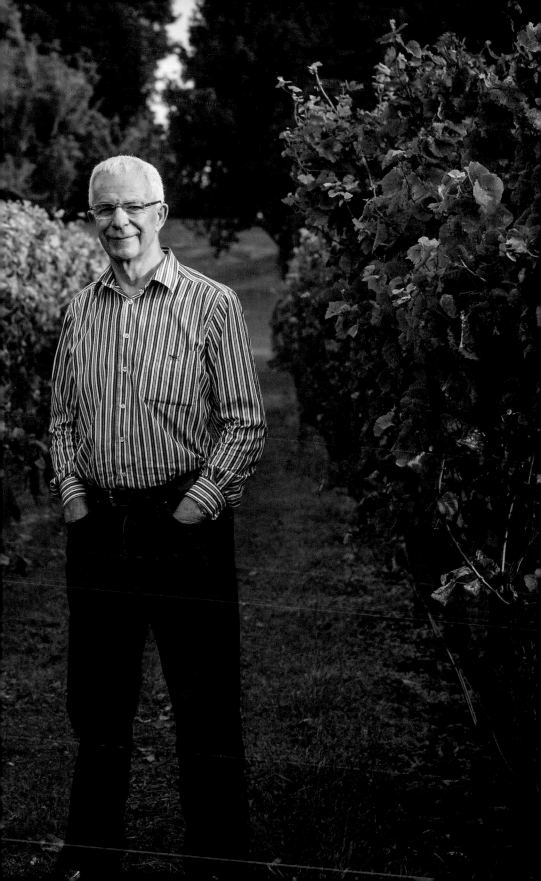

*As the new millennium dawned,
Villa Maria was doing well and
George was healthy and happy.
With the stress and anguish of
the 1980s now well behind him,
and with the huge export success
of the 1990s, it seemed that Villa
Maria was well placed to face
whatever challenges might arise.*

A very good night at the 2011 awards. Back row,
from left: Oliver Powrie, company viticulturist;
Alastair Maling, general manager winemaking and
viticulture; George Fistonich; Karen Fistonich;
David Roper, Auckland winemaker; Nick Picone,
senior Auckland winemaker; Jeremy McKenzie,
senior Marlborough winemaker. Front row: Murray
Cook, Marlborough winemaker; Craig Thomson,
Marlborough grower viticulturist; George Geris,
chief Marlborough winemaker.

In 2000 Montana had purchased Corbans, and the following year was itself taken over by international drinks giant Allied Domecq; not long after, it would become a part of the huge Pernod Ricard empire. Cloudy Bay, the high-profile Marlborough company established by Australian David Hohnen, became part of the Louis Vuitton–Moët Hennessy empire, which meant New Zealand's largest wine producers were by the early part of the decade controlled by the French.

But the French were not the only ones to have influence in the way the New Zealand wine industry was progressing. The large Australian wine producer BRL Hardy had purchased Nobilo's and Selaks, and later it would be sold to the world's largest wine company, Constellation Brands, which already owned Kim Crawford and which is based in the United States. Overseas money was also represented by individual investors who had established wine companies in New Zealand, either by investing in existing operations or establishing new ventures. By the late 2000s, many well-known brands believed by many to be New Zealand companies were in fact wholly or partially overseas-owned. These included Craggy Range, Corbans, Te Awa, Trinity Hill, Wither Hills, Dry River, Escarpment, Fromm, Matua Valley, Kim Crawford, Stoneleigh, and many others.

It's a matter of some pride to George that Villa Maria has remained privately and New Zealand-owned. And in 2001 he once

LEFT
George with his
Ernst & Young
Entrepreneur of the
Year trophy.

ABOVE

George receives the Distinguished Companion of
the New Zealand Order of Merit, the equivalent
of a knighthood in the period when New Zealand
had abandoned honours, from then Governor
General Dame Silvia Cartwright in 2005.

Ian Clark dressed as town
crier, and the staff gathered to
hear his cry, at a surprise staff
gathering before George and
Gail flew to Wellington for
George's investiture in
2009 as a knight.

again became the sole shareholder when he was able to purchase the last 10 per cent he did not already own.

Since 2004, recognition for George and the company he founded and has nurtured for more than 50 years has flowed thick and fast. In 2004, *National Business Review* named George Fistonich its New Zealander of the Year. This was followed in 2005 by his being named the first New Zealand Wine Personality of the Year. That same year he was named Ernst & Young New Zealand Entrepreneur of the Year, going on to represent New Zealand in the World Entrepreneur of the Year contest in Monte Carlo in 2006. Villa Maria was named New Zealand Wine Company of the year for the seventh time in eight years at the 2005 Australian *Winestate* magazine awards.

But arguably the most high-profile award came in 2005, when George was awarded the title of Distinguished Companion of the New Zealand Order of Merit, the equivalent of a knighthood. However, it wasn't until the government reverted to the previous honours system and once again allowed those with awards to use the accompanying title that George became 'Sir George' and Gail, Lady Fistonich. His investiture was on 14 August 2009, when he flew with Gail to Wellington to be formally invested by Governor General His Excellency Sir Anand Satyanand. It was the first-ever knighthood to be accorded a member of the New Zealand wine industry.

IN 2005 GEORGE bought Marlborough's Thornbury vineyard, established by Steve Bird and Bruce McCutcheon in 1997, in yet another effort to increase his supply of grapes. Bird had been assistant winemaker to John Hancock when Hancock was with Morton Estate, and had a reputation for producing quality wine from the grapes grown on the Thornbury estate. George decided to keep the brand, appointing Simon Fell to the winemaker role. Thornbury now produces regional wines such as Pinot Noir from Central Otago, Sauvignon Blanc from Marlborough, Gisborne Chardonnay, Waipara Riesling and Bordeaux-style wines from Hawke's Bay.

So impressed were judges at the prestigious Royal Easter Show

Wine Awards in 2009 that they awarded a gold medal to the Thornbury Merlot 2007 and Silver to the Thornbury Pinot Gris 2008. Australian wine judges have also endorsed Thornbury wines, giving four stars to the Thornbury Gisborne Chardonnay 2008 (*Winestate* 2009).

The years since 2005 have mostly been good to Villa Maria. Bumper harvests have meant that there have been none of the grape-supply issues that plagued the company throughout the 1970s, 1980s and the early 1990s. The company finances are in good shape, and domestic sales — in spite of the high-volume, low-price imported wines flooding the supermarkets — have continued to grow. But George, never one for resting on his laurels, continues to tinker with the way Villa Maria operates, forever looking for ways to streamline operations and to introduce management efficiencies that he believes reflect business best practice.

'I am still fascinated with finding how best to sustain a company of this size into a long-term successful company,' he says. 'We have been approached to sell on more than one occasion. But we have never seriously considered any of those approaches. We have survived for more than 50 years through some really tough times, and after all this effort it would be nice if we can get an iconic New Zealand company like Villa Maria to stay family-owned. I realise it's quite a goal, but if everyone buys into it, it is definitely achievable.'

Achieving the same level of commitment from all stakeholders to the preservation of Villa Maria as a family-owned company has led George down a number of organisational paths in recent years, some of which are based on business management principles he has discovered through his reading or through exposure to companies he sees as being particularly successful.

In 2008 he presented a case for significant cost savings to the board. The board suggested that staff would be more engaged in the process if suggestion boxes were placed throughout the business, with an incentive of $1000 being paid for the suggestion that saved the company the most money. George was not entirely convinced of the need for the incentive, but he felt that getting staff on side

The Villa Maria concert
series has starred many
international acts. Here
George poses with Tom Jones.

was imperative, and so he eventually agreed. The scheme collapsed within six to seven months, in large measure, George believes, because there were no management systems in place capable of sustaining it.

In 2010 a further set of cost-saving measures was put in place; measures that resulted in more positive results. But George was still not convinced that he had the organisational structure he wanted. 'I felt bad because I was asking people to commit to cost saving. There was a bit of discontent, and I felt like killing it, but I knew I couldn't. I knew what the end goal was, but I somehow felt we were still not organised and needed more time. We had reduced the costs as far as we could, so it was more about efficiencies. So we kept on.'

Something of a watershed occurred in late 2010 when, during a strategic planning session involving the senior management team, everything seemed to come together. 'We looked out into the future,' says Fabian Yukich, 'decided what we wanted to achieve over the following five years, and set ourselves 10 major goals. As part of that we decided to adopt the "Lean" approach to management.'

Lean is a business management tool which Toyota in Japan — where it's known as *Kaizen* — had developed for its manufacturing processes. It has since evolved into Lean thinking, a widely accepted management concept that allows companies to look at how they can add value to their dealings with customers by close analysis of ways to reduce waste and inefficiency.

George brought the Lean concept to the board after seeing it in action at boat-builder Alloy Yachts. It seemed to him to tick all the right boxes. 'They had five bays for building yachts that were in various stages of implementing Lean processes. Because the roll-out had been gradual, you could see concrete evidence of the improvements the system was making, by comparing the bays part-way through the conversion with those that were 100 per cent up and running. I was impressed by how everything was spotless — the floor was spotless, the tools were all there and it was a pleasure walking through it and must have been a pleasure working in it. More importantly, as we talked to the management team I learned how it encompassed the whole business and how all the staff were involved. I immediately knew that this was the kind of environment I wanted for Villa Maria.

'One of the key things about Lean thinking is getting rid of waste, whether it is wasted materials or wasted time, especially searching for tools and for information. Apparently people spend anything from five to eight hours a week searching for files or information. When you think about how competitive it is out there, you know that you cannot sustain a business for long with that kind of statistic. I suppose it also fits in well with my Croation upbringing. We were not very well-off and basically had a culture of not being allowed to waste anything, especially time.

'I got out of receivership because Villa was super-efficient and had a passionate and committed staff. But I have the impression that efficiency is something people find hard to get. About 25 years ago it seemed like I was buying a new screwdriver every week. There was always somebody nagging me to buy a new screwdriver, and I reckon that I must have bought about a dozen screwdrivers, so I decided I was not going to buy any more screwdrivers. Next time I was asked I made everybody stop for an hour and we went searching. We found 12 screwdrivers. It's a similar situation now. When we adopted Lean the production team went through the production area and found it was a mess. They put a red flag on all sorts of items — boxes, disused labels, even on an old bloody bicycle — and sent it all off to the tip, truckloads of items. Now there is a board for everything and it is all marked. It sounds silly, but it's simply housekeeping and it makes everything much more efficient. It has to become part of our long-term culture.'

The current restructuring is a huge undertaking, involving around 200 of the company's 300 staff on all four sites. Its implementation is in the hands of Villa Maria national operations manager Robin Collis, with Fabian Yukich and group chief winemaker Alastair Maling also playing key roles. George, as ever, is intimately involved.

'I know as leader I have to be passionate about these things, as they're critical to our future in this very competitive industry. And I find it easy to be. I try to make sure I plan my time and any travel around the meetings, and if there is any possible way of being involved I will cut my trip short so I can be there, at least some of the time. It's one of those things where I have to show my support.'

Overarching the project is the mantra 'Achieving Continuous Excellence' (ACE), which the team decided best sums up the goals they want to reach. The project is now two years into implementation, and Yukich believes it is already paying dividends. 'We have always been reasonably well organised, but this takes it to the next step and makes it very visual. It begins with a form of house-cleaning when you simply get rid of all unnecessary clutter. It's called the Five Ss: sort, set in order, shine, standardise and sustain. The second aspect is value-stream mapping, where you take a whole process and you map out every part of that process, and you find the milestones within that process where you need to make a decision before the next thing can happen, and you make sure you are getting those milestones right.'

Yukich says debate and discussion are critical to the success of the exercise, but George clearly remains the most influential participant. Nowhere was this more evident than during the second phase of the restructuring, when the team was required to select a project which would serve as a template for using across the business. George had strong opinions.

'Robin Collis and some of the others initially wanted to apply the mapping process to our biggest product, Private Bin Sauvignon Blanc, which is our biggest seller,' George remembers. 'I said, with white-winemaking, particularly Sauvignon Blanc, it is relatively simple, and even though it is important to get those processes right, we needed a first project that covered all aspects of winemaking. So after quite a bit of debate, because it all has to be a shared vision and process, we decided on Cellar Selection Pinot Noir, because the grapes for this wine are both hand-harvested and machine-harvested, the wine goes into old barrels and new barrels, and the wine goes through virtually every single winemaking and marketing process the company has, and sales are to a whole range of local and export markets. It meant that the template would extend beyond the Auckland and Marlborough

George collects another prize
at the 1994 Sydney International
Wine Awards.

Long-time staff members on the bottling line,
from left: Christine Nukunuku, Ngaire Samuel,
Bella (Elizabeth) Nathan, Mary Lee Te Young,
Joanne Nathan and Henry Samuel. Villa Maria
operations manager Fabian Yukich is at far right.

plants and also cover the other wineries — Esk Valley, Thornbury and Vidal — because it picks up all those processes, and so that more staff would be included.' The others agreed.

Villa Maria is the first New Zealand wine company to institute the Lean approach at such a level, and while its full effect is yet to be felt, George believes Lean is a prerequisite for survival. 'People who are using it say they are saving 20 to 40 per cent off their overheads, which means that any wine company that does not get into it will find it hard to survive because it's now about efficiencies as well as making top wine.'

The scope and scale of the project is no barrier to George's enthusiasm. 'It's bloody huge because of the amount of work to get it working. The guy who is running it for us says that the hardest part is bedding the changes into the culture so that it becomes the way Villa Maria does business for the rest of its life. So this project actually has to last forever. I'm very excited about the way we are getting total commitment from all our people, and how they are enjoying it.'

'OUR PEOPLE' IS APT. George Fistonich is the sort of boss who cares about his employees, who invests in them, and who leaves a mark on them. Not all of them are undying fans, but it would be fair to say that most of them are. They're people like Rebecca Poynter, who started working for Villa Maria in 1995 as one of the first two national account managers, and who now manages a wine company in the Hunter Valley.

She was hired at a time of real growth and change within the business. 'Suddenly we were using AC Nielsen, had a full-time analyst on-board and were actively analysing sales,' she remembers. She also quickly came to realise that she was in an industry that dealt with a horticultural commodity. 'I started in April, at vintage, and that year it rained. And rained and rained. Trucks of over-saturated Sauvignon Blanc grapes were backed up at the contract processing plant in Marlborough. Wineries were wondering how they would cope with an overly large vintage of potentially average-quality wine. But not George Fistonich. As usual, George had a plan. When you've got more wine than you can sell, what do you need? More reps, of course. I was one of them.'

She is one of many Villa Maria employees who got a big break with George. 'George later confessed that nobody else in the company wanted to employ me. My CV wasn't great. Too many past jobs; I might have seemed a bit unstable. But for some reason he decided to give me a chance. Having said that, he thought I'd either be very good or very bad. Six months would tell. Around about 10 years later I think he finally admitted he was wrong!

'In our lives we are lucky if we have someone who gives us a break, who inspires us and who becomes a mentor. George has been that to me. But I am not alone. Scratch the surface of so many wineries and wine businesses, not only in New Zealand but also much further afield, and you will trip over a winemaker, viticulturist, marketer or sales person all of whom got a start at Villa Maria or who have worked there at some point in their career. From my era alone there are numerous general managers, chief winemakers, company viticulturists, consultants, international wine judges, Masters of Wine and marketers dotted around the globe who started their career at the Villa Maria, Vidal or Esk Valley wineries. The environment George Fistonich creates at his wineries has a lot to do with their success.

'George has always done things his way, and his way has more often than not been different to others. His focus on training and development meant that in my time with the Villa Maria sales and marketing team I often went to five or six conferences a year. These were no "junkets", but they were certainly never boring! We did it all, from relatively traditional sales training, such as Dale Carnegie, to conferences where we were led through creative visualisations. We "crossed silly bridges", created our own "best selves", role-played difficult meetings with buyers, and even held hands and sang "That's What Friends Are For"! But no matter what direction the conference took, George's objective was always to encourage his team to think outside the square. We were challenged to rethink how we did our jobs and then to develop initiatives and strategies for success. We left empowered to do better than our competitors. I have no doubt that this level of investment in people has been a key factor in the success of Villa Maria.

'Now I manage a team myself, and every day I find myself thinking and acting on things I learned from George. Things that I didn't really know I knew until it came to put them into practice. I think of them as "Georgisms". Georgisms include putting candidates through rigorous psychological testing, while still using his astute observation of everyday behaviour to help draw conclusions about how people will perform on the job. George once told me that he would be disappointed if I didn't get thrown out of at least one sales call, because, unless I was pushing it, I wasn't doing my best. George was always happy for us to make mistakes, so long as we learned from them — and, of course, didn't repeat them!

'I joined Villa Maria in the mid-1990s, and by that time the company had been around some 35 years. Wine was relatively new in the grocery channel when I joined. Independent trade and retail liquor chains were significant volume-drivers as opposed to the more niche position they hold today. But things were about to change fast. After a couple of years selling into supermarkets without too much pressure, suddenly wineries needed to understand the principles of category management and how to deal with supermarket buyers the way other grocery segment suppliers had always.

'Back then it was often commented on by the trade that George employed a lot of women. He had already employed the first female wine rep in the industry, and by the time I was part of the team he had a second female as sales manager, Angela Lewis. Both of his first national account managers were women — Anne Fenwick, who later went on to become marketing director for a major wine distributor in the United Kingdom, and me. We also had a very talented female winemaker, Michelle Richardson, and numerous "girls" out selling and promoting Villa Maria wines. I didn't discover until a few years later that in the trade his sales team was known by many as "George's girls" — which I like to think of as the Kiwi equivalent of "Charlies Angels"!

'I left the Villa fold for a couple of years in 2000 to develop my marketing skills, and was delighted to be given the opportunity to return in 2003 as the first group marketing manager. Two years later I left again for Sydney to develop both the Australian and Asian markets. Villa Maria entered the Australian market well after many other New Zealand wineries, yet has managed to grow solidly both in my time and since. That success is thanks not only to good distributors, but is also a testament to the relentless pursuit of quality by the company's winemakers and viticulturists which has delivered much success in national wine shows. The wine trade and consumers alike have embraced the Villa Maria brand as a result.

'I am privileged to have shared over 10 great years of Villa's 50-year journey to date. I am very grateful for the opportunities the business gave me. For me, Villa Maria is all about the great people who choose to work there. People who continue to make Villa Maria New Zealand's most-awarded winery. And at the heart of it all is George Fistonich, whom I can't thank enough for putting me on the path that is the wine industry, and for showing me a different way to look at both work and life.'

Villa Maria Wines ready for
tasting in at a Wok+Wine wine
tasting event near the Brooklyn
Bridge, New York City, during
George's roadshow through the
United States in 2012.

19

A MILESTONE

2011 marked 50 years since George Vjeceslav Fistonich persuaded his father Andrija to lease him the five acres of land and the shed in which Andrija had built a rudimentary winery to make port and sherry to sell, and a few bottles of basic wine to enjoy at the family table.

George and Gail at a
reception in Shanghai,
during George's 2012
roadshow to mark Villa
Maria's fiftieth vintage.

When George formed Villa Maria Wines in 1961 he was 21, and the New Zealand wine industry was in its infancy. New Zealanders were not the wine consumers they are today, yet there were plenty around who, like George, saw a future for making wine here.

Already established throughout the country was a range of small wineries producing red and white wines from a limited selection of grape varieties. For the most part it was the immigrant community that was at the forefront of winemaking. But that was changing. The winemaking environment was being heavily influenced by constantly evolving liquor laws, the desire of the beer brewers to protect their turf, and, perhaps most importantly, the development of a restaurant culture.

It was in this environment — where the only constant was change — that George went about building Villa Maria Wines. Using borrowed money and a great deal of intuition, he made decisions others considered foolhardy: he experimented with new grape varieties; he persuaded growers to sign contracts that rewarded quality as much as quantity; and he was passionate about customer service, which led to an unanticipated spiral of growth. It wasn't that success was a happy accident; it was more that he was not the sort of businessman driven by grand 10-year plans. Above all, he backed himself.

Nick Picone, who joined
Villa Maria in 1997 as a
cellar hand, was appointed
Villa Maria's senior
winemaker in 2012.

Along the way he attracted both admiration and scorn. He became the focus of a campaign by big-business investors in the industry to rid it of small companies, leaving the market to a very few big producers; he lost his company to the banks but re-established it in record time. And through sheer determination he has expanded what was literally a backyard business into the fifth largest wine producer in the land. As George says, 'First in quality in all our four tiers of wine, and still family- and New Zealand-owned.'

Villa Maria Estate is by far the most-awarded wine producer in the country. The company has received a level of international recognition few, if any, have managed to achieve, and George is the recipient of personal accolades that no one else in the New Zealand wine industry has earned.

At the 2011 Air New Zealand Wine Awards, Villa Maria was accorded special recognition for having had won 60 trophies over the 25 years the awards have been running, making it the single most awarded winery in the history of the competition. Included in its haul have been four Champion of the Show awards; two for Chardonnay and two for Pinot Noir. At the same competition it was announced that Villa Maria had won the Champion Wine of the Show with the Single Vineyard Keltern Chardonnay 2010, a repeat of the feat achieved in 1987, when the company won the very first Champion Wine of the Show for its Gisborne Chardonnay.

Even for a company used to winning awards in wine competitions, 2011 was a stellar year for Villa Maria. For the first time ever, one company had won the coveted Champion Wine of the Show Trophy at every New Zealand wine competition in a single year. It is an impressive list:

- 2011 Royal Easter Show Wine Awards — Villa Maria Reserve Syrah 2009
- 2011 Speigelau International Wine Competitions — Villa Maria Ihumatao Chardonnay 2010
- 2011 Bragato Wine Awards — Villa Maria Single Vineyard Keltern Chardonnay 2010
- 2011 New Zealand International Wine Show — Villa Maria

Single Vineyard Keltern Chardonnay 2010
* 2011 Air New Zealand Wine Awards — Villa Maria Single
Vineyard Keltern Chardonnay 2010

That's quite a medal haul.

2011 was also the fiftieth anniversary of another enduring and critical relationship: the marriage of George and Gail Fistonich, which George and Gail celebrated with a trip to Paris and Sicily. Gail Fistonich has been an integral part of George's success, has been privy to his disappointments, shared his tribulations, endured his anguish, tolerated his idiosyncrasies, offered advice, raised his children, and experienced the consequences — good and bad — of his decisions. She knows him better than anybody.

IT'S APRIL 2012, and on the first floor of the business heart of Villa Maria's stylish Mangere complex, a small group of staff is meeting to discuss how best to celebrate George's fiftieth vintage. George is there; there can be no show without Punch. So are those whom he trusts to come up with some appropriate way to remind the world of what a great family-owned company Villa Maria is, how it remains the most awarded winery in the country, and why New Zealanders should continue to support it.

Local celebrations are planned for October 2012. They are to involve dignitaries, influential wine commentators from overseas, suppliers and, of course, staff current and from the past. It is to be a party, just like the parties of old; the parties George and Villa are famous for, with great food and plenty to drink.

Celebrations are also planned in countries around the world where Villa Maria wines are so popular. These will involve the company's agents and supporters, as well as the all-important international wine media. Already, George has been out in the world, on a three-stage, six-month, fiftieth-anniversary tour of all Villa Maria's markets, meeting distributors, customers, the media. In May he'd been in the United States, Canada, China, Hong Kong and Japan, on a punishing schedule that featured lunches and degustation dinners and tastings and media interviews. When he rose to speak at each event he wove the Villa Maria story through New Zealand's story. He talked about this country's great olive oils, wine, seafood and coffee culture. This was the place, he said, where you could get the best flat whites and cappuccinos in the world. He described the fantastic vineyard cafés the country's wineries offered, from the top of the North Island through to Central Otago. How visitors could go fishing, skiing, sailing and bungy-jumping. And he mentioned that there was a great and comfortable airline that could get visitors here: Air New Zealand. 'Audiences always love this talk,' he smiles. 'I'm passionate about the importance of selling New Zealand and helping our tourism industry. The wine industry is a great medium to achieve this. I encourage all my winemakers to remember what a great country we live in and to spread the message.'

Before October he would be off again, this time to Australia, and then to Finland, Holland, Belgium, Bulgaria, Russia, Ireland and the United Kingdom, where Villa Maria would be a sponsor at the BAFTA Awards dinner in London.

Meanwhile, in the meeting, George lets everyone have their say, listens, nods in agreement, and then reminds them to make sure they have plenty of media present. This is a great opportunity to once again tell the Villa Maria and the New Zealand story.

After all, it is the remarkable tale of a remarkable man who is much admired by his peers, by the wine community, by industry observers, and even by those who have, over time, had cause to question his relentless and often unconventional approach.

The fiftieth-vintage anniversary celebrations will last at least six months, and George will be enthusiastically involved in every aspect of the planning and the implementation — as always.

Gail and George in China in
2012, at a dinner organised
by Villa Maria's distributor
in China, Summergate.

APPENDICES

Gail and George in 1986
at the House of Commons,
London, where they
collected Villa Maria's first
ever international award.

A SELECTION OF WINE AWARDS

- 1963 Royal New Zealand Easter Show: Villa Maria's first ever awards — a second and third prize for Villa Maria Burgundy and Villa Maria Red Table Wine, respectively
- Record for most trophies (60) over 25-year history of Air New Zealand Wine Awards
- International Wines and Spirits Competition, London, 1986: Trophy for the Best Gewürtztraminer, Villa Maria's first major International award
- Sydney International Wine Competition: Most Successful Winery 2007
- *Restaurant Wine* magazine (USA): Winery of the Year 2006
- International Wine and Spirits Competition (London): New Zealand Wine Producer of the Year 2004, 2006 and 2009
- New Zealand Wine Society Royal Easter Wine Show: Trophy for Most Successful Exhibitor 2000, 2001, 2002 and 2004; Trophy for Champion Winemaker 1993, 1997, 1998, 2001, 2002, 2004 and 2005
- *Winestate* magazine (Australia) Awards: New Zealand Winemaker of the Year 1999, 2000 and 2006; New Zealand Wine Company of the Year 1998, 1999, 2000, 2002, 2003, 2004, 2005, 2006, 2007, 2008 and 2009
- Liquorland Top 100 Wines Competition: Champion Winery of the Year 2001, 2003, 2004, 2006, 2008 and 2009; Champion Wine Producer of the Year 2008 and 2009
- *Wine Spectator* magazine (USA): Critic's Choice Award Winner 2000, 2001, 2002, 2003 and 2005
- *Wine Enthusiast* Annual Wine Awards (USA): New World Winery of the Year 2007

- Intervin International Wine Competition in North America: Andrew Sharp Award for Excellence 2000
- Villa Maria voted producer of New Zealand's best wines overall by members of Cellar Masters, New Zealand's leading wine club, 1997 and 1998
- Villa Maria has a record three out of four wines chosen for the prestigious BBC *Food and Drink* television programme 1997
- New Zealand Wine Society Royal Easter Wine Show: Champion Winemaker 1993, 1997, 1998, 2001, 2002, 2004, 2011
- New Zealand Wine Society Royal Easter Wine Show: Highest number of gold medals 1997 (8), 1998 (7), 1999 (3), 2000 (4), 2001 (10), 2002 (10), 2003 (6), 2004 (10), 2005 (10), 2006 (13), 2011 (17), and 2012 (11)
- Air New Zealand Wine Awards: Highest number of gold medals 1999 (8), 2000 (5), 2001 (6), 2002 (6), 2003 (12), 2004 (14), 2005 (14), 2009 (15), and 2011 (16)
- Sydney International Wine Competition: Champion Wine of the Show, beating 1000 wines from six countries, 1997
- International Wine Academy (Australia): Trophy for the New Zealand Winemaker of the Year 1987

VILLA MARIA
AND SPONSORSHIP

VILLA MARIA'S EARLY promotional efforts were all about getting the public introduced to wine, which meant sponsorship was often directed towards groups that presented opportunities for tasting wine, especially where there were willing tasters — sports teams, beauty contests, surf clubs and so on.

It was only when positioning of the brand became more important that sponsorship of the arts and more high-brow events became George's focus. The earliest significant sponsorship of this sort was of Auckland's Mercury Theatre, which closed in the late 1980s. Other arts-group sponsorships include the New Zealand International Festival of the Arts and the Manukau City event Cult Couture.

Current sponsorships include: Auckland Philharmonia, Auckland Theatre Company, New Zealand Opera, the Michael Hill Violin Competition, The Halberg Trust, the *Cuisine* New Zealand Restaurant of the Year awards, Ernst & Young Entrepreneur of the Year awards, Art Works, the Vodafone Music Awards (Thornbury), the Salasai Fashion Awards (Vidal), the Mayoress's Ball, and local marae, schools, sports clubs and other organisations.

Sir George was the charter chairman of the Mangere Lions Club and is the patron and benefactor of the Variety Club of New Zealand. Villa Maria also assists many organisations every year with donations of wine for fundraising and events.

CHIEF AND SENIOR VILLA MARIA WINEMAKERS

Villa Maria Estate – Auckland

1962–1967	George Fistonich
1968–1973	Ross Spence (went on to co-found Matua Valley Wines)
1974–1975	George Fistonich
1976–1982	Harry Wright
1982–1985	Mark Polglase: chief winemaker (went to Penfolds Wines and Montana before returning to Villa Maria Estate in 2009 to become cellar door manager)
1985–1992	Kym Milne MW: chief winemaker (now a consultant winemaker based in Australia)
1993–1995	Grant Edmonds: chief winemaker (went on to form his own wine company)
1998–2002	Michelle Richardson: chief winemaker (went on to form her own wine company)
2002–2008	Cory Ryan: senior Auckland winemaker (went to McWilliams Wines in Australia)
2002–2012	Alastair Maling MW: formerly chief winemaker and now Villa Maria general manager winemaking and viticulture
2008–present	Nick Picone: senior Auckland winemaker

Former Villa Maria chief
winemaker Alastair Maling, now
general manager winemaking
and viticulture, with trophies at
an awards dinner.

Villa Maria Estate – Marlborough

1999–1999   George Geris / Jules Taylor (went on to start her own wine company)

2000–present   George Geris: current chief Marlborough winemaker

Vidal Estate

1976–1987   Warwick Orchiston (started with Seppelt Vidal in 1971 and stayed on after George purchased the company in 1976)

1987–1990   Kate Radburnd (went on to become chief winemaker and shareholder at CJ Pask Winery)

1990–1997   Elise Montgomery (now a Hawke's Bay wine consultant)

1997–2006   Rod McDonald (went on to form his own wine company and wine consultancy in Hawke's Bay)

2006–present   Hugh Crichton: current winemaker

Esk Valley Estate

1987–1988   Robbie Bird (George purchased Glenvale Wines from the Bird family)

1990–1992   Grant Edmonds (transferred to Auckland winery to become chief winemaker)

1993–present   Gordon Russell: senior winemaker

Thornbury Wines

2005–2006   Steve Bird (George purchased Thornbury wines in 2005, with Steve Bird as winemaker)

2006–present   Simon Fell: current winemaker

LONG-TIME EMPLOYEES OF THE VILLA MARIA FAMILY

Bella (Elizabeth) Nathan
Bella has worked for Villa Maria for more than 25 years, firstly between 1979 and 1988, leaving when her youngest child was born and joining again in 1996. She works in the rework and special label section in production, and has a meticulous eye for detail.

Joanne Nathan
Bella's eldest daughter, Joanne, began with the company in 1994 as a process worker on the bottling line. In 2002 she was promoted to the production supervisor role.

Mary Lee Te Young
Mary Lee began working at Villa Maria Estate in October 1983. She was actively involved in the decommissioning of the old bottling line when the Kirkbride Road winery was expanded in the 1980s, and now in her role of production hoist driver she ensures there is order on the end of the packaging line.

Ngaire Samuel
Ngaire joined Villa Maria as a process worker on the production line in 1994. In her 18 years with the company she has worked her way up to her current position as inwards goods supervisor. Ngaire says she has met and worked alongside many wonderful people and witnessed

many changes at Villa Maria. She hopes to continue working in the company and being part of Villa Maria Estate's future success.

Henry Samuel
Ngaire's brother Henry began employment with Villa Maria in 1995 as a process worker in the production area of the company. In 1998 he was moved to the line setter's role, before being promoted to night shift supervisor and then on to his current role as production technician.

Christine Nukunuku
Christine joined Villa Maria in February 1994, working initially in a quality-control role in the winery laboratory. She then moved into production quality control, before becoming production manager and also performing purchasing duties for the production section. Further promotion saw Christine taking on the role of planning and purchasing manager before being appointed to her current role as purchasing manager.

Dave Field
Dave started working at Villa Maria as a cellar hand in November 1998, before being promoted to cellar manager in September 2000. Critically important to the company, Dave's mechanical knowledge, attention to detail and focus on quality have seen him involved in many of the company's major projects, from the setting up of new bottling equipment to an active role in the setting up of the cellar at the new Auckland winery, and helping new winemakers understand the winemaking process.

Mary Winstone
Mary began with Villa Maria in 1998, originally as the sole receptionist and as support for Sir George's personal assistant. She is now receptionist and guest co-ordinator, and her role includes preparing itineraries and hosting international inbound guests referred by the international market managers.

Steve Sykes

Steve joined Esk Valley Estate in 1988 and is currently cellar manager. Steve knows every aspect of the operation of the Esk winery, and is valuable not only for his skills in the cellar but also for his huge knowledge of the plant and equipment used in the winery.

Peter Winter

Peter joined Esk Valley Estate in 1988 as a cellar hand and engineer, and is now engineer for Esk Valley Estate and Vidal Estate. Peter's abilities range from concreting through to carpentry and steel fabrication.

Sue Cranswick

Sue joined Esk Valley Estate in 1991 and has been cellar door manager since 1993. Sue's bubbly personality and devotion to the wines of Esk Valley have made her a legend around the cellar doors in the Hawke's Bay. In 2004 at the Hawkes Bay A&P show she won the Mercedes-Benz Cellar Door Personality of the Year Award. In 2008 she won the Hospitality Awards Personality of the Year Award.

Winemaking team

George Geris

George started with Villa Maria as assistant winemaker at the Kirkbride Road site in 1997. With the building of the Marlborough winery for the 1999 vintage, he spent the 1999 and 2000 vintages based in Marlborough running the winery. George became Marlborough winemaker and relocated permanently to Marlborough in early 2001. He later became senior winemaker, and has held his current position — chief Marlborough winemaker — since 2008. George manages the Marlborough winery, site and team, and oversees the Marlborough wines. 2012 is George's fifteenth vintage with Villa Maria.

Nick Picone

Hawke's Bay local Nick Picone started with the Villa Maria group as a teenager working as a cellar hand at Esk Valley Estate in 1997. After several vintages he shifted to Marlborough as Villa Maria assistant winemaker. He remained in Marlborough for four years, eventually becoming winemaker. Nick then moved to Auckland to take on the role of senior Auckland winemaker in 2008, co-ordinating all of Villa's North Island wines. Having completed international vintages in California and Italy, 2012 marks Nick's 16 vintages and his thirteenth with Villa Maria. He was appointed chief winemaker in 2012.

Phil Holden

Phil joined Villa Maria in 1999 and is now vineyards manager for Gimblett Gravels (Ngakirikiri, Omahu and Twyford Gravels). During his time with the company, Phil has developed and planted all of the Twyford Gravels vineyards, as well as a large portion of Omahu Gravels. He oversees all of the above vineyards, as well as all Pellenc machinery for the company. He also manages the company's machine-harvesting for Hawke's Bay.

Vince Edwards

In 2000 Vince started working part-time in the cellar door while studying winemaking and viticulture at the Nelson Marlborough Institute of Technology. After graduating, Vince worked in the winery and cellar door, becoming the cellar-door manager in 2002. Over the years Vince has subsequently taken on the duties of PR manager for Marlborough, sales rep for on-premise accounts, events planning, hospitality and Pinot Noir winemaker during vintage, as well as promotional work in the USA.

David Roper

David's first vintage with Villa Maria was in April 2002 when he was a part-time cellar hand at the Kirkbride Road winery. He started full-time in October 2003, before becoming assistant winemaker in 2005 and subsequently Auckland winemaker two years later, in 2007. David works closely with the Villa Maria senior winemaking team to ensure wine is produced to specification and delivered to bottle in a timely manner. He has special responsibility for the wines from the Ihumatao Vineyard and, in conjunction with the cellar manager, manages the winery cellar team.

Alastair Maling MW

Alastair is Villa Maria's general manager winemaking and viticulture. Born and raised in Hawke's Bay, Alastair completed a commerce degree at Lincoln University but was drawn to a career in winemaking. After working a vintage in Hungary, Alastair returned to New Zealand to complete a Postgraduate Diploma in Oenology and Viticulture at Lincoln University in 1994, after which he worked a vintage at Esk Valley Estate. Between 1995 and 2002, Alastair travelled extensively throughout the old and new world wine regions, gaining a wealth of experience with an impressive range of grape varietals and international winemaking styles in France, California, South Africa, Spain, Chile and Argentina.

In 2000 Alastair became the sixth New Zealander — and the second only New Zealand winemaker ever — to pass the prestigious Master of Wine exam. In 2002 he returned to New Zealand to take up the position of group winemaker at Villa Maria Estate. As group winemaker, and more recently as general manager winemaking and viticulture, Alastair is responsible for the viticulture and winemaking of all the group's wine brands. He sits on the Villa Maria senior leadership team and is heavily involved in overseas market visits.

In 2003 Alastair was named by *Decanter* wine magazine as one of five young New Zealanders to 'watch out for' in the wine industry. He has also been honoured with the title of Winemaker of the Year at the Royal Easter Wine Show in 2004, 2005, 2008 and 2011.

Alastair was awarded the White-Wine Maker of the Year trophy at one of the world's most highly regarded wine competitions, the International Wine Challenge in London, in 2007.

Aside from his viticultural and winemaking duties, Alastair also served on the Gimblett Gravels committee from 2003 to 2006. In 2007 Alastair joined the board for New Zealand's own Pinot Noir Conference. He has subsequently chaired Pinot Noir 2010 and is the current chairman for Pinot Noir 2013.

Simon Fell
Joining the Villa Maria family in 2003, Simon is currently winemaker for the Thornbury range, co-ordinating, planning and creating the six varietal wines in Thornbury's portfolio. Thornbury produces regional wines from New Zealand's top five grape-growing regions: Marlborough, Hawke's Bay, Gisborne, Central Otago and Waipara. Simon travels extensively and often represents the entire Villa Maria portfolio in international markets.

Michaela Rush
Michaela began with Villa Maria at the Marlborough winery in 2003 as a vintage cellar hand, and then became part of the permanent winery staff in Marlborough. Michaela took on the role of systems winemaker in 2008, a role that involves her in many aspects of winemaking, quality systems administration, staffing and logistics.

Hugh Crichton

Following an early change in career direction from commerce to wine, and a 12-year period abroad, Hugh returned to New Zealand and joined Vidal Estate in 2004. Leading the winemaking team since 2006, 2012 is his eighth vintage with Vidal and eighteenth in New Zealand and abroad.

Jeremy McKenzie

A born and bred Southerner, Jeremy has a wealth of winemaking experience in new and old world wine regions. He began work as a winemaker with Villa Maria in Marlborough in 2006. In 2008 he was promoted to the role of senior winemaker, and is now responsible for a large number of Villa Maria's Marlborough wines, from vineyard to bottle. In addition, Jeremy travels extensively internationally, representing the Villa Maria portfolio. He is also well known for his hunting, diving and fishing exploits, and his cooking of wild game and its matching with wine in the interest of building lifelong supporters of Villa Maria.

TOP

George and his elderly Fordson
truck on a grape-delivery run.

ABOVE

Another sort of truck; Villa Maria
used this vintage truck for
promotional work in the early 1980s.

LEFT

Some very early and innovative
packaging, complete with
screwcap closure.

LEFT

Longtime Villa Maria staffer
Ian Clark clowns around
at an awards event.

BELOW

The Family of Twelve.
From left: Paul Brajkovich (Kumeu
River), Ivan Donaldson (Pegasus Bay),
Judy Finn (Neudorf Vineyards), Steve
Smith (Craggy Range), Phyll Pattie (Ata
Rangi), Richard Riddiford (Palliser
Estate), Clive Weston (Nautilus Estate),
Ross Lawson (Lawson's Dry Hills), Annie
Millton (The Millton Vineyard), Blair
Walter (Felton Road), Pol Lenzinger
(Fromm Winery) and George Fistonich
(Villa Maria).

LEFT

Sir George and Gail,
Lady Fistonich.

BIBLIOGRAPHY

Cooper, Michael, *The Wines and Vineyards of New Zealand*, Hodder & Stoughton, Auckland, 1993.

Cooper, Michael, *Wine Atlas of New Zealand*, Hodder Moa, Auckland, 2008.

Courtney, Caroline, *Wine in New Zealand*, Random House, Auckland, 2003.

Scott, Dick, *A Stake in the Country: Assid Abraham Corban and His Family, 1892–2002*, Reed, Auckland, 2002.

Scott, Dick, *Pioneers of New Zealand Wine*, Reed, Auckland, 2002.

Stewart, Keith, *Chancers and Visionaries: A History of Wine in New Zealand*, Random House, Auckland, 2010.

Thompson, Joelle, *Celebrating New Zealand Wine*, New Holland, Auckland, 2004.

INDEX

ACKNOWLEDGEMENTS

GEORGE FISTONICH AND KERRY TYACK wish to thank the many individuals who were interviewed for this book, including: Gail, Lady Fistonich; Karen Fistonich; Elsie Thom (neé Fistonich), to whom we are especially grateful for her in-depth research into the early history of the Fistonich family, her recollections of the Fistonich children's upbringing in Mangere, and the early days of the Croatian community; Maurie Servantie; Mike Aspros; Mark Polglase; Peter Howell; Ian Clark; Angela Lewis; Kym Milne MW; Rod McDonald; Drazen Mijatov; Elise Montgomery; Rebecca Poynter; Michelle Richardson; Grant Edmonds; Ross Spence; Fabian Yukich; Sue Bird; Steve Bridges; Bob Campbell MW; Steve Smith MW; Terry Dunleavy MBE JP FWINZ; Kate Radburnd, and Debbie Gilchrist.

A CLOSING NOTE

NEW WINE COUNTRIES need heroes. They may be braggart and swaggering. They may be silver-tongued masters of persuasion. They may be tyros whose brilliance hurls undreamt-of flavours high into wine's firmament. Or they may operate below the radar for years, innovating, pushing the boundaries, so that when the chance to take the lead appears, they're good and ready.

George Fistonich crept cautiously onto the New Zealand wine scene in 1961 when he released Villa Maria Hock into a less than ecstatic marketplace. Over the next 25 years, he massively expanded his company, nearly lost it once as he tried to fight the big boys in a brutal discount war, and got it back through sheer bloody-mindedness. That was 1985, and that was the last time George would let Villa lose sight of quality as its ultimate goal.

Quality at a fair price. Villa would never be the cheapest, but, despite being showered with gold medals and trophies over the next 25 years, it was never the most expensive either. George's genius is that he understands that consumers do crave quality. They will pay the fair price.

Despite being a global brand, there's a family feeling at Villa which George assiduously fosters while ensuring that his team produces some of New Zealand's tastiest yet most affordable wines. That's because he tells his winemakers to follow their vision of flavour, to make the best they can make. And through astute vineyard planting and close partnerships with growers, he makes sure they have the best grapes to work with. Sounds simple? Then why don't more large companies do it?

George doesn't shout about his ideas or his achievements, but they keep coming. When I first went to Villa's amazing new winery near Auckland, George said, 'This is designed for 50 years hence.' He paused. 'We've had 40 years to learn from our mistakes.' And as he turned away, did I hear him say: 'And I haven't wasted any money'? When you've been as close to the abyss as George has been, and clawed your way back, you don't waste money. But invest $30 million in the future of Villa Maria and the future of New Zealand wine? That, he'll do.

Oz Clarke
London
July 2012